How To Throw Fabulous Parties On A Budget

Lori Perkins

For more information contact:
Riverdale Avenue Books
5800 Arlington Ave.
Suite 18J
Riverdale, NY 10471
www.riverdaleavebooks.com

Design by www.formatting4U.com
Cover by Scott Carpenter

Digital ISBN: 9781626017474
Trade Paperback ISBN: 9781626017481

Second Edition, May 2026
First Edition, 1999, published by Kensington Books as
The Cheapskate's to Entertainment: How to Throw Fabulous Parties on a Budget

Riverdale Avenue Books would like to thank you for reading this copy of *How to Throw Fabulous Parties on a Budget* by gifting you one free book from each imprint, which you can download at the link provided:

www.preview.mailerlite.io/preview/1098983/sites/136486432257607665/0kJ9TD

To my dad,
Who taught me the fine art of frugality

And to my mom,
Who taught me the love of entertaining

And to my son,
Who celebrated many of these parties with me
and inspired many more

Table of Contents

Introduction

I wrote this book more than 25 years ago, when I was a young mother and just starting out in my career in publishing. A quarter of century later, I am surprised at how relevant it still is, and how the information I gathered and the lessons I shared are even more useful now that we are entering another time where we have to do belt tightening.

I am now at the end of a successful literary career, and scaling back as I prepare to retire, yet I am still an avid party thrower and goer. My life has changed as I went from being a young mother to a single mom to a divorced senior citizen, but I still believe that gathering friends and family together to celebrate the ups (and downs — I've now coordinated a few memorials and funerals, as well as divorce parties) of life are the true joys of existence.

This book will hopefully guide you through some of the most important life markers, as well as inspire you to be your creative, frugal best and share those celebratory moments with the people you love, like, and work with and still have money left over to do it again!

Lori Perkins,
May 2026

Introduction

All my life I've been a tightwad. It's a personality trait that I acquired from my dad, who did the family food shopping and knew no greater thrill than double coupons and "buy one, get one free" (BOGO). He sought out early bird specials and restaurants that served a free glass of wine or after-dinner drink with the meal. He taught me to wait until the holiday sales to make big purchases (such as cars and appliances), to travel off-season whenever possible, and to comparison shop on every item I could ever want, including my college education and my wedding.

My mother taught me the joys of entertaining. We have a large extended family and have always had family get togethers for the holidays, even when times were tight. My parents had a large crowd of friends and they entertained at least once a year at what I thought of as elegant cocktail parties. I loved to watch my mother putting together trays of mushroom and sausage hors d'oeuvres, that we were not allowed to touch.

I went to a fancy private school (on scholarship, of course) where the birthday parties were held at Broadway shows in midtown Manhattan hotels, but my mom managed to throw me equally impressive parties at a fraction of the cost of those of my classmates by being more creative than my friends' parents. Even before I had a place to host parties, I was throwing them for my teenage friends when my parents would go away for the weekend. I would put together disgusting punches based on two bottles of Southern Comfort (which, in addition to being all I could afford, was known to be potent) and vats of onion dip and chips.

It was only natural that when I became a young adult and moved out on my own, I was the party girl. Of all my friends I could always be counted on to throw the Halloween party, the annual New Year's Eve party, and the Thanksgiving feast, even though we all made less than squat (we were starving journalists).

As newlyweds, my husband and I continued the tradition of New Year's Eve parties; we threw my brother his going away to California party and even organized a treasure hunt throughout Manhattan for our friends one summer. I threw my parents a surprise 25th wedding anniversary party (my dad nearly had a heart attack, so the surprise part was not such a good idea) and my husband and I each gave the other a 30th birthday party. (Plus I threw him a surprise 35th).

We're parents now, so we do our child's birthday party, as well as the annual holiday gatherings for the extended family and a whole summer of weekend barbecues for our friends, because we live in New York City in a co-op with a pool, and most of our friends have no place to swim.

Over the course of the year, we host about ten parties and another dozen dinner gatherings. Most are simple and intimate dinners at home for fewer than 12 people but this year I threw an office party for 120 as well as a very complicated child's birthday party for 14 children and their parents with an *Indiana Jones and the Temple of Doom* theme.

I love to entertain, and I love being the one to bring all my friends and family together for a good time. Even though we are a two income family, we could never throw the parties we do if we didn't plan everything and squeeze blood from stones to put everything together.

Not everyone is a natural cheapskate, but few of us can afford to do all the things we want without pinching pennies here and there. It takes a certain mindset to constantly figure out ways to save money, but it is one that can be easily learned.

Many of my friends say they can't afford to entertain as much as we do, but that's because they overdo it and exhaust both their financial and time budgets in doing so. Entertaining is an important part of who I am, so I actually budget it into my life. I plan to entertain on a regular basis, and I'm therefore not surprised by how much it cost or how much time it takes to prepare and clean up.

I know that we will be hosting at least 25 get together every year, so I always keep my kitchen well-stocked and buy entertainment-oriented items, such as paper plates, and plastic cutlery in bulk. If I had to, I could throw together a dinner party for 16 or a buffet for 30 at the snap of a finger on next to nothing, or for less than $25.

One time I did have to. We hosted a christening luncheon for our son, and several members of the immediate family came back to the apartment with us, and stayed until dinner, for which I was roasting a relatively small leg of lamb (to serve eight). I threw on pots of rice and made a killer salad and ended up feeding at least 16 people. I made it all look effortless.

The goal this book Is to make entertaining so affordable and effortless—and thus enjoyable—that you can't imagine a weekend without some kind of party!

October, 1999

Chapter One: The Basics of a Successful Party

It is easy to entertain extravagantly. There are very few guess who would not enjoy a meal of filet mignon, caviar and fine champagne. There are also very few of us who can afford to serve that meal to more than six people more than once or twice a year. I wouldn't want to either, because it would be the luxuriousness of the ingredients, and not my contribution to them, that would make the biggest impression.

For me, the success of any gathering is in the personal details—the place (I've chosen to invite you to my home), the choice and distinct flavor of the food, the ambience, décor, and company. With enough planning and careful attention to detail, you can make any party seem truly extravagant without spending yourself into bankruptcy.

I strongly believe that all gatherings should have a theme. It gives a unifying concept to your party and a direction for your creativity. A theme makes it easier for you to decide what to cook and how to decorate, as well as how to set the tone for your gathering. It gives the hostess a focus around which to plan the perfect personal details.

When I look back on the most memorable dinners and parties I've attended, I rarely remember whether or not the hostess served on Limoges china, or had a Waterford crystal punch bowl. It was often the simplest things such as a homemade ethnic feast or special event, like a treasure hunt, that made a lasting impression.

Years of hosting parties have taught me that various decisions must be made and carefully thought out well in advance. For example, do you want to have a sit-down or buffet dinner or cocktail party? Is there a theme for the party? What is the basic menu? Do you want to have any special ambiance and décor? Once you've decided upon these party basics, then you move on to the organization of budgeting of the party.

Deciding What Kind of Party

For me, the kind of party I'll choose to have depends on the number of people I can fit comfortably into my apartment and how much work I want to do once my company arrives. I can fit 12 adults at my dining room table and a children's table very comfortably, so 16 is my maximum for a sit-down dinner, though there is the option of placing another table in my living room and rearranging furniture. I once attended a sit-down Christmas dinner where the furniture has been completely removed from the living room, and four tables were placed in an open square to seat 40, which worked quite well.

For more than 15 people, and up to 30, I would have a buffet dinner, where I present the food on my dining room table. I might add a small table or two for drinks or dessert. This way, I can serve sumptuous meals that come in individual portions, such as a carved roast or chicken Parmesan.

For more than 30 people, and up to a maximum, for my home, of 60 (which is the maximum I would recommend for the average three-room entertainment area of interconnecting dining room, kitchen, and living room), I would host a cocktail party. This would require at least two large tables at opposite ends of the party area, and small tables of finger food distributed throughout.

Deciding on the Menu and Theme

Most of the gatherings we host are for a specific occasion, such as a birthday or holiday. Many of them come with a pre-planned menu because of family tradition (turkey on Thanksgiving, lamb, or ham on Easter) or because they always fall at a certain time of year (someone's summer birthday is always a barbecue). However, it Is easy to vary the menu or the theme with just a little creativity. If you find yourself hosting a number of Christmas gatherings, for example, try something like a Christmas fiesta where you serve Mexican food, and perhaps feature a Christmas piñata for the children.

The theme can be expressed by something as simple as deciding to have Italian food (antipasto, a pasta dish, and Italian pastries supplemented by an Italian wine and music), or as complicated as hosting a vegetarian low-fat birthday for someone with a health issue (grilled fish and vegetables, an angel food birthday cake with white and gold accents and perhaps an angel motif).

Putting together the theme of a dinner or party is relatively easy. It's just a matter of coordinating the food and decor and ambience according to some unifying concepts. As in the examples above, you can do this by choosing to serve a certain type of food (French, Chinese, Mexican), by occasion (holiday or birthday), by season (barbecue or picnic), or by an idea you come up with on your own (a '70's or Star Trek party). You can go through the basic elements of a party, such as food, décor and entertainment, to make sure that they all coordinate.

While the food I serve is often decided by the theme of the party, I try to also take into consideration what's on sale seasonally, such as fresh picked apples in the fall or basil or blueberries in the summer. Turkey and leg of lamb are more readily available around the holidays (less expensive too). The supermarkets that I frequent have seasonal sales on filet mignon or lobster tails, so for a New Year's Eve party we serve fillet mignon (everybody is asked to bring supplements to the main course). In New York City, St. Patrick's Day is a big holiday, so corned beef is on sale for two weeks at $1.99 a lb. (when it is usually close to $10 a lb.). I buy four, host a corned beef and cabbage dinner for my friends who don't cook, and make the rest into corned beef hash. Sometimes I base the theme of the party on the food, instead of the other way around.

Decor and Ambience

Once you know what you are going to serve, it is easy to set the table. As long as you remember to keep an eye open for elegance and/or creativity, you should be able to put together a unique and decorative table, using color, texture, and whimsy, without spending a lot of money. A well-set table should feature a centerpiece of some sort (this can be very simple), a table covering (this does not need to be traditional table linen), and accents, such as candles and candlesticks, or flowers.

Your home should reflect your taste and style. If you are comfortable with your home, your guests will be too. Never try to present a style that is not comfortable for you. For instance, if there is not a single white feature in your home décor, you should not feel compelled to run out and buy white table linens. You'll be more comfortable if you find a tablecloth that reflects your taste. The same goes for china and flatware.

I have found that the table centerpiece can often be put together from the food you are serving. A basket of highly polished apples or a bowl piled high with summer fruit is as beautiful as an antique vase of pink roses. In the fall, I often put together a centerpiece of autumn vegetables, such as squash, pumpkin, and corn, around a basket of fresh baked bread. For Easter, I place hand dyed Easter eggs in a ceramic basket as the table centerpiece.

Because I often set my table centerpiece from what I am serving, I have a made a habit of collecting baskets—from my son's Easter basket rejects to those that come as gifts with toiletries. Lined with a linen napkin or even a colorful dishcloth, they make wonderful accents, when filled with bread, fruit, wildflowers, colored eggs, or holiday cookies. Near the holidays (which includes Valentine's Day), you can pick up almost any size basket (from unvarnished to gold sprayed) at the dollar stores.

I've also collected a number of bowls, from a large pasta bowl to small, condiment-size dishes. I tried to find them in colors and patterns to complement my everyday dishes but I will also buy glass or crystal dishes, because they go with everything. I have a special four-section glass dish in which I serve olives and pickles, and I use it almost every time I entertain.

For a table covering, you can use the more traditional lace or linen tablecloth. However, more creative table coverings, such as a handmade quilt or large piece of fabric (batik, or even muslin) or color-coordinated materials to go with the holiday or season (red and green for Christmas or pastel for spring or Easter) make very nice accents. Some hostesses choose to dress up a plain table with a decorative runner, which can be a seasonal or colorful pattern.

Table accents can be as simple as matching candlesticks, whether family heirlooms, or dollar store finds. Ceramic figurines are also a nice touch for holidays, and they can be as expensive as Lladro or as inexpensive as pilgrim figurines found at an outlet store.

I also have a few nice vases (one was a wedding gift, one a flea market find, and one I made—see chapter three) in which I will occasionally place seasonal flowers. I love to display pussy willows in the spring and wildflowers all summer. A few well-chosen silk flowers (which I've seen on sale at the dollar store) make a good investment for last-minute decorating, as well as all-year-long floral decoration.

In addition to dressing up a table with food filled baskets, large seashells make interesting holders for condiments. Some caterers swear by hollowed out red and green peppers or purple cabbages as balls to hold dip.

I have invested in some nice salt and pepper shakers (a crystal set, as well as silver), as well as a handful of seasonal shakers (for Christmas, Halloween, Thanksgiving, and Easter), because they also dress up the table.

Music is important to set the tone of the evening, but it should always be in the background, unless you are having a party with dancing. For ambience, I often play classical music, or jazz, or Spanish guitar, but I will always play holiday music when appropriate.

If the basic elements of your party are well thought out, and you are proud of them, you will give off an air of confidence, which will ensure that your guests are comfortable. When your guests are happy, and you are self-assured, your party is bound to be a success!

Chapter Two: The Basics of Frugal Entertaining

The single, most essential way to save money is to *plan ahead.* While it is possible to throw a much talked-about party on a whim, you're bound to spend much more than you have to if you don't take the time and make the effort to think everything out advance.

Attention to detail is the second most important element of successful entertaining on a budget. You must cover all the entertaining basics, and then pick one or two party elements and really splurge there, such as on a fabulously rich dessert, or a complicated appetizer. Your guests will remember for years that you served homemade stuffed artichokes or a lush array of strawberries dipped in chocolate and never recall that the china didn't match or that your glasses weren't crystal. Choosing the right details with which to make your personal entertaining statement is essential.

When to Start Planning

A month is a good time frame to give yourself, although I often plan for annual parties (my son's birthday) or holiday get-togethers all year round. By this I mean, I'll begin collecting coupons for the holiday feast in August (I often buy holiday accents the day after the holiday, when they are usually half price--tablecloths, candles, salt and pepper shakers, ceramic figures) and, once my son has decided on the theme for his annual party (Star Wars, Batman, Aladdin, Power Rangers, Indiana Jones), I immediately begin collecting party favors and assorted paraphernalia.

Allowing yourself a month also gives you enough time to send out invitations (everything is emailed today) and get back responses so that you'll know how many people will be coming. There is nothing more embarrassing than not having enough food, beverages, or party favors and running out to the store at the last minute. On the other hand, you don't want to get stuck with too much food that you can't return and six extra party bags for five-year-olds. A month also gives you ample time to shop around to get the best buys on the things you will need to look for those "just so" details that will make your party stand out. It should also give you enough time to set up to help you might need.

The Importance of Lists

Make a list of everything that's involved in planning the party. Don't expect that you'll just remember to go out and get ice the day of the party or that your friend will remember to return your big salad bowl on time. You need lists to plan the menu and figure out how much food you need, as well as how much liquor, soda, and ice to have on hand. Make sure you have enough dishes and cups (with extras for refills), flatware, table linens, and napkins, garbage bags, and paper towels.

You also need to make a list to help you plan your décor, if you are going to need any centerpieces, candlesticks with candles, banners, or party favors. This is especially important if the party is for a special occasion (you do not want to be searching for birthday candles or something to light them with at the last minute).

Be absolutely sure to make a list of things to do the day of the party and the order in which you will do them. This ensures that you won't forget some detail like putting the beer on ice and that you won't be in the middle of setting the table when the doorbell rings.

Budgeting Time and Money

You have to set realistic budgets for both time and money, and have a fallback plan (such as taking off work the day before the party, if necessary) in case either one of these projections goes dreadfully wrong at the last minute. It is my firm belief, and one that has been proven true throughout my part-throwing life, that you can get anything you want or need at a discount if you just take the time to shop around. However, this may mean going to 10 different stores and then back again for the best price. Only *you* know if it's worth it.

I do a lot of bargain shopping online and follow it up with phone calls.("Do you have Batman party plates? How much are they?"), so I don't have to go from store to store. You'd be surprised how easy it is to do the research and make the calls, but it does take time, which you have to budget. Of course, Google is not going to tell you if your local dollar store has Star Wars party favors, so you might have to make a list and put aside some time to make some calls.

However, once you locate what you want, you may even be able to get some of your party supplies delivered by Instacart, but make sure you key in your membership ID to get all your discounts. Using Instacart may also make getting things into your house easier, so consider that as well when budgeting. It might cost you more for delivery, but time is money.

I also always try to buy as much as possible the weekend before the party.

Liquors are often the most expensive element of a gathering, so the type and quality of drinks you serve will largely determine how much you spend overall. Champagnes and expensive wines might be what you choose to splurge on, but you can make just as impressive a statement by serving champagne punch, or an unusual wine (such as Beaujolais Nouveau, which arrives in the States from France the third Thursday in November), or make pitchers of mixed drinks. You can always buy wine by the case or in larger bottles (and serve in decanters or pitchers) so your guests don't know you bought the four-liter jug of sangria and just added fruit slices.

The main course is the second biggest factor determining the cost of the party. Expensive cuts of meat and shellfish will cost you a pretty penny, but you can save money if you look for sales. (Get friendly with your butcher, and he or she may tell you about sales ahead of time). Other ways to save up are by buying in bulk (sides of beef to freeze, large quantities of filet mignon or shell steak, roast your own pig, cutting your own meat--a full chicken is cheaper than chicken breasts), or buying frozen. Frozen African lobster tails or Chilean shrimp are fine for something like paella. You could also buy one expensive ingredient, such as crab, or smoked salmon, and stretch it out by serving it in a pasta dish, soup, or bisque, or a salad as the main course. I once had a fillet mignon salad that was out of this world.

Appetizers and dessert are usually not budget busters but you can choose to splurge here with something like caviar and brie appetizers and toast points (a little caviar and a lot of brie) or some truffle hors d'oeuvres. Some desserts are more expensive to make than others, such as those that require liqueurs (but you can buy small bottles) or hard to find fruit.

Budgeting time to shop properly and to make all these exquisite menu items is essential. When I entertain, I only have one or two difficult and/or time-consuming menu items, which I prepare the day before (usually the dessert, maybe the bread). I make a lot of batches of things all year long, such as pesto and pie crust and sugar cookie dough, so I just defrost it when the time comes. I like to save the day of the party for setting up and preparing the main course.

Where to Shop

I live in New York City, so the world is my oyster, but the places I shop for party goods can be found throughout the country, especially in suburbia. One year, I found the entire party set up for my son's Aladdin-themed birthday at a party store that was going out of business on vacation in Florida. I bought the whole lot (centerpiece, tablecloths, goody bags, balloons, and blowers) and carried it back to New York in a shopping bag. My husband thought I was crazy, but my son was in his glory, and the party was a big success, because the details were perfect (the other moms were amazed that I had managed to find a genie piñata).

Of course, you can find so much on the internet today as well. If you have memberships that entitle you to free shipping (Prime and Walmart, for example), you might try searching there first. You can also shop for goods at Partycity.com (free shipping after spending $50). Oriental Trading has been a party shopping favorite and essential for me for decades. Archee McPhee has an extensive selection of oddball party supplies. And a lot of dollar stores and discount stores have party supplies and ship.

I go to different stores for different kinds of party supplies. I might drop by my local TJ Maxx or Home Goods for a more elegant party and FiveBelow or OddLot for something more seasonal or casual (all of these stores are online now too, but I do love the hunt).

For food and beverages, I will usually go to my local wholesale membership store (Costco, BJs, Sams). I find that the annual membership fee is far less than what I would spend if I didn't shop there, especially since I host a number of parties a year (I also buy other household items and my son's lunch supplies in bulk all year round). You can also find discounts online to join these clubs on Groupon and other sites .And if you don't want to join, you can ask around to see if you can borrow a friend or family member's card or offer to share a membership (most of these are for two people). And, as I mentioned, if you are buying a lot, and it's heavy (such as many 2 liter bottles of soda or water bottles), you might opt to use Instacart so you don't have to load and unload everything in and out of the car and to your home.

I find these wholesale clubs are great for getting large amounts of food, especially the more expensive cuts of meat, and fish and fancy ready-made appetizers. (smoked salmon, hummus, pate, wheels of cheese). They're also good for fruit and vegetables in bulk. I often buy Italian bread, pizza, and French bread, and freeze them for the day of the party.

The stores are also a good place to buy assorted crackers, but I find I can sometimes get better deals at a supermarket on the better brands of chips and snacks. This is an area where you have to comparison-shop.

Some wholesale clubs feature hors d'oeuvre platters, from shrimp cocktail to crudites with dip, as well as charcuterie plates, which could really save you time and money, but you must buy them the day of the party.

Costco doesn't sell liquor in New York, so I go to a Costco in New Jersey for party liquor. (There is also no bottle deposit in New Jersey, so I save on cases of soda and/or beer, and the sales tax is slightly less, but tolls have risen rapidly in the past decade, so this only works if I am buying a lot). You can also search online for the discount beverage or liquor store nearest you.

Of course, I go to supermarkets for most of my every day food needs (dairy products, flour, coffee, tea), and some of my meat. I prefer to go to a green grocer for my fruits and vegetables, because they have more variety and the produce is usually cheaper and fresher. For instance, I can always get two lemons for a dollar at the local green grocer, whereas they're up to a dollar each at the supermarket. Bags of potatoes and onions are often less expensive as are herbs and spices.

Go to a specialty store (such as Zabar's or Balducci's in New York, or even a Whole Foods or a Wegman's) only for specific items, such as gourmet coffee beans or a hard-to-find-cheese or spice. Supermarkets generally have extensive sections of ethnic food where you can usually find the basic ingredients for Latin, Greek, Italian, Thai, Chinese and Japanese food. Many Italian specialty ingredients such as marinated mushrooms, peppers or artichoke hearts, and pine nuts, can be found in bulk at a wholesale club at a good price. For specific ethnic ingredients, I prefer to go to a local ethnic shop such a good as a Greek or Italian deli, where these items are more likely to be cheaper.

I am addicted to dollar stores, where every item in the shop is supposed to be a dollar (but now many dollar stores have raised the price to $1.25 or $1.50, but mostly still worth it). I've never been to a state that doesn't have one, and I travel extensively throughout the east and the west coast every year. Most are in malls and have the words dollar or $.99 in their name. Do not be shy about asking friends, family, or co-workers where the nearest dollar store is.

I also shop pretty religiously at discount stores such as FiveBelow, Ocean State Job Lot, Odd Lot, Lot Less, Big Lots, and Renys (in Maine). They often have holiday and party supplies at deep deep discounts. Many of these stores are now online too, which means their wares are available to everyone, not just locals.

After a holiday (New Year's, Valentine's Day, Easter, Fourth of July, Halloween, Thanksgiving and Christmas) the big box stores (Target, Walmart), pharmacy chains (CVS, Walgreens, Rite Aid) and supermarkets put their seasonal décor (and candy) on super sale for as much as 90% off (I once got a bag of Valentine's-themed chocolate truffles for $.90 at Stop & Shop). If you know you throw an annual holiday party, this is a good time to buy party supplies and décor such tablecloths and knick knacks. This is how I bought my annual Pilgrim salt and pepper shakers, as well as my Christmas cocktail glasses.

Don't' forget eBay and Etsy. On eBay, you might be able to buy the left-overs from someone else's themed party at a fraction of what it would cost new (as long as they are new in box--NIB). It's always worth a search to see what might be available when you search your theme and the word "party." Etsy will offer you original created items, many of which you can use as centerpieces for much less than what you might pay for a mass-produced version from a Big Box Store.

And you should always do a search for "sale" or "clearance" items on the online stores of your themed party, such as Disney or Universal, as well as on pop culture sights such as Hot Topic.

If you don't mind getting a lot of email (I have a separate email address just for mailing lists), you might want to sign up for newsletters, because they often come with coupons, as well as limited time sales.

Coupons, Discount Codes and Deals

When I was a young mother, I used to keep a coupon file, but times have changed. Now most coupons can be downloaded on an app. I always sign up for the supermarket membership cards, which give you the discount when you type in your phone number. When I'm throwing a party, I will often browse the weekly flyer online to see what deals are currently being offered. A lot of BOGO sales are perfect for charcuterie spreads or appetizers. Aldi and Lidl are particularly good for this.

Groupon also has some interesting discounts on strange things like M & M's with individual letters on them, so browse there before you purchase anything.

It is worth your time to search on the web for discounts just by typing in the place you are interested in purchasing from, such as "Carvel" and the word "discount" or "sale." There are often discount codes and coupons you can download if you only take the time to look.

Many supermarkets also offer free food if you spend a certain amount in a period of time at certain times of the year (spend $250 from Nov. 1-20th and get a free turkey). One year, I earned a free turkey at Christmas, a smoked ham at Easter and a five-pack of Matzoh for Passover. For the Fourth of July, you will often find BOGO sales on hotdog and hamburger buns. I freeze everything and then use them when I entertain.

Bartering and Borrowing

I am a great fan of barter, and by this, I mean exchange of services. For example, a friend who makes a wicked German chocolate cake will make you one in exchange for your babysitting her three kids one afternoon. You'd be amazed at what you can barter if you set your mind to it. Sometimes by bartering, you're giving someone a chance to hone their skills and use you as a future reference. (Let's say a neighbor's teenager is learning jazz guitar, and you could use some musical entertainment…)

I also believe in borrowing with payback, but the payback can be in services or a future IOU on something you can lend. Don't buy an extra pot or coffee machine; borrow it, and let your neighbor use your printer. However, you should never borrow without expecting to return the favor.

Negotiating

As a literary agent, I make my living negotiating, so I'm never embarrassed to say that I don't think something is priced fairly. However, I find many of my friends feel ripped off because they don't even try to negotiate for services and find out after the fact that someone else got the same service cheaper.

Just about everything is negotiable, from wedding receptions to kids' parties. Most of the time, all you have to do is ask, and the salesperson will tell you the ways in which you can cut back on the price (have the party on Friday night instead of Saturday, pay cash, book early).

Negotiating takes a little preparation. You need to do some research online as well as make some calls so you know the going rate, and you also need to set a fairly firm budget in your head.

My company recently held a catered party for 120 people, where we decided to feature cold food, which is cheaper (see Chapter 4 on catering). In the first round of calls we made to inquire about price per person for cold cuts and dips we were told $15 per person, which was too much. When we asked how we could cut the cost, a handful of caterers said we couldn't, but most offered to simplify the menu (just roast beef and turkey with two cheeses) or suggested serving a large sandwich, and we were able to cut the cost in half.

I can't tell you the number of times I received a quote for a "firm" price from a caterer, but found that after I said a competitor would charge less, there was suddenly an amazing amount of flexibility about what could be offered. This happened in the case of a midtown Manhattan hotel reception with steak and an open bar as well as a child's christening reception. Caution: make sure at the outset that there won't be any extra charges for setting up, delivery, rolls, salads, etc. All of this should be gone over in the preliminary negotiations.

Yard Sales, Flea Markets and More

Yard sales, flea markets, rummage sales, swap meets, thrift shops, and garage sales are a gold mine for those who entertain frequently. You can often pick up extra household and holiday items at a fraction of the cost.

You would be surprised how many people don't know where to look for these sales. Most people forget that the local neighborhood paper is an excellent source of information: it will list most church and institutional sales by date, as well as announce tag, estate, and sometimes yard sales. People also forget that the local thrift shop or Salvation Army store is a treasure trove.

When I first started visiting the sales, I was constantly overwhelmed by all the fabulous junk that was offered. I would either buy too much, and then not be able to use it, or regret that I hadn't bought those beautiful green goblets because I was being cheap that week. To eliminate these sources of remorse, I have begun to keep a wish list of things to look for at these sales on my iPhone. I look at my list before I enter. I update my wish list—a kind of entertaining inventory—on a regular basis. I know what I don't need, so I won't be liable to buy another coaster set or salt and pepper shaker when I already have too many.

Below is a very basic list of items I look for at flea market:

Table linens
Silver serving pieces
Large bowls (Crystal is nice)
Glass sets of 8 or 12
(can be used for dessert)
Chaffing dishes
Candlesticks
Pitchers
Coasters (holiday or seasonal)
Crystal or sliver salt and
pepper shakers
Fancy china pieces
(Lenox, Wedgewood)

If you don't have the basics, flea markets are a good place to buy the following:

Stack Tables
Crock pot
Serving trays
Silver tea set
Juicer
Small food processor
Hors d'oeuvre trays
Punch bowl and cups

I often go straight to the person who is organizing the sale and ask if they have the items I am looking for. Often they do, but they haven't put them out yet. You can also ask the local thrift shop to keep an eye out for a certain item for you and give them your phone number.

Using Creativity

Details make all the difference in truly memorable entertaining. It is not how much you spend on a party, but how do you make use of what you spend. If you have the time, you can probably think your way out of any bond you might come up with by using creativity, and remembering that great entertaining is always in the details.

My rule of thumb on this is to choose one or two details and really go whole hog. For instance, a typical potluck dinner might feature the basic pasta, salads, bean salad, and chili dishes, but you can dress the whole thing up by ordering platters of large shrimp with cocktail sauce as an extravagant appetizer.

Some of the best parties I've ever been to probably did not cost a lot to throw, but the hostess put an enormous amount of time and creativity into them. For example, one mom put together an Alice in Wonderland Mad Tea party for her six-year-old daughter, and made all the decorations herself (copying the famous Tenielle illustrations onto napkins and tablecloths). She also made up games that went with the theme and then gave out miniature tea sets as party favors.

Some of the best adult parties I've ever been to have been the ones where I've had to bring my own booze. At one memorable party I had to put my share into a kitty that went for a pair of Broadway tickets for the winner of a treasure hunt. One hostess called to ask each guest to make his or her very best dish for eight—what a scrumptious meal!—and she supplied an exquisite table setting and expensive wine. A cocktail party where we were served martinis and macadamia nuts stands out in my memory as well.

Details are best when they're homemade (and cheaper that way too). You can make just about anything you might need from scratch, from appetizers, to cakes, linens, and decorations. If you need help, the best place to go is the Internet. Use your favorite search engine and type in one or two words that will describe what you're looking for such as "Thanksgiving recipes" or "birthday parties."

You can also go to the library for books on holiday and party decorations, or look online for back issues of some of the more creative women's magazines for recipes and arts and crafts ideas.

Taking the time to come up with one or two creative details for your party will ensure that the event is remembered and will make your guests feel that you went out of your way for them.

Chapter Three: Party Basics at Home

Home entertaining is a lot of fun if you are comfortable with your home. I find home creates a much more relaxed ambience than hiring a hall and caterer or even going out to a restaurant with a group. However, it is also a lot more complicated.

One of the most important elements of home entertaining is making your guests feel welcome, and that you are enjoying their company. You can't do that if you are loading the dishwasher or making a complicated glaze. You have to make a real effort to organize your meal in such a way that there is always time to talk to your guests. This is one instance where the planning of the meal, and the cleanup in between courses, is vitally important. Without adequate planning, you'll spend your whole party running from the kitchen to the dining room without ever finishing a sentence.

Whether you're having just another couple or 60 people (probably the maximum for home entertaining with comfort), you'll have to make a few decisions at the outset.

Preparing for Company

You should set aside the day before the party (or the night before after work), to make the house as spotless as possible. If you've always been meaning to clean fingerprints off the woodwork, this is the time to do it. Even if your guests don't notice, you will and will during the entire time of your party. Same goes for stains on the rug, which can easily be removed with spot cleaners.

If you have anything it would kill you to see damaged or broken, put it away, because accidents always happen. When I had my brother's moving-away party, I moved all my living room furniture into the bedroom, so that the guests could dance. One of the guests had too much to drink, went to lie down in the bedroom, missed the bed, and fell on my antique, mahogany coffee table and broke it. One of my guests at a New Year's Eve party threw a glass from my new crystal set against the wall to ring in the new year because that's what they had done in her country. If children are coming, assume that they will get into everything and move your Murano glass vases or Precious Moments figurines to a china cabinet. There's nothing more difficult than trying to assure your guests that the sculpture your husband made of you on your honeymoon can be glued back together or that your Snow Babies collection can be easily replaced. It ruins the party for everyone.

The best thing to do to prepare for children is putting out little dishes of popcorn, chocolate kisses, and M&Ms, things they can get easily into. These goodies should keep them away from the caviar and pate, which they probably won't like. Some adults will go for this stuff too.

I also warn my child that other kids are coming. I tell him to put away the toys that he does not want to share or that he would be upset about if they broke.

Put away the things you do not want your guests to become preoccupied with. I have an aunt who keeps her wedding album under the glass of her coffee table. She always complains that people who come to her house look through it and comment on how thin she was years ago. That wouldn't happen if the wedding album was out of public view.

The same applies to anything you don't want to share with your company. I have an uncle who collects 50 year-old Metaxa and is upset when someone comes to his house and drinks it (one guest *did* drink an entire bottle). If it wasn't displayed prominently in his liquor cabinet, no one would know it was there.

If people can smoke, either tobacco or vaping, in your home, you have to share your smoking policy--"smoking is permitted on the terrace" or "in the backyard" or "my co-op forbids smoking indoors."

If you're going to be using special dishes, or grandmother's china, wash all the dishes and glasses the night before the party (you can check for chips this way too). If you're going to use silver, make sure it is polished ahead of time. This is not the sort of thing you should be doing as the food is cooking.

Planning the Party

If you're having less than 10 people, can invite them over the phone via text. For any more than that however, you should send out invitations.

How fancy or informal they are is up to you and the occasion, if any, you are celebrating.

You can use many of the free online services such as Evite, Partiful or Punchbowl. You can create some really clever or whimsical invitations this way. These computer invite sites also allow you to include things like directions, as well suggestions for things to bring (which really works well for a potluck) and electronic RSVPs. They also give you the opportunity to send out a party reminder days before the event. And you can send out a thank you this way after the party.

Planning the Meal

The kind of party and food I serve depends on how many people are coming. As I said, my dining table comfortably seats 12, and I can put up to four kids in the nearby kitchen (I believe in a kids' table), so 16 is the maximum for a sit-down dinner in my home. You should calculate the comfortable maximum in your own home, and either borrow tables to sit more or serve dinner as a buffet which is what I recommend once the guest list climbs above 16.

If I'm serving a sit-down dinner, I always serve a roast (unless it's St. Patrick's Day—then it's corned beef and cabbage). I do these well, and my guests all seem to love them. Roasts are easy to cook and still relatively inexpensive. Turkey is very cheap between November and January (sometimes as little as $.69 a lb.). Leg of lamb is usually on sale in the spring, as is smoked spiral ham. Since roasts just need to be seasoned and then popped in the oven for a few hours, with occasional basting, I'm left with plenty of time to work on the side dishes and appetizers.

When I shop, I am always on the lookout for a well-priced piece of meat, because I entertain about once a month. There's usually a turkey in my freezer and I will always buy a leg of lamb if it's on sale. Roast pork and ham are favorites as well. However, if you haven't bought a roast ahead of time, you can always go to a wholesale club and buy a roast at a good price.

In the summer, it is easy to vary the menu with a sumptuous, seafood pasta meal, such as grilled tuna in olive oil and garlic or shrimp. Scampi over pasta paella works well too.

I like soups in the summer as well. I cold gazpacho or light egg and lemon soup is a nice way to start a meal.

Since so many people are vegetarians, as well as have food-related issues, I make at least four side dishes—usually mashed potatoes in the winter and potato salad in the summer (a 5 lb. bag of potatoes should run about $1.99), lettuce and tomato salad with Nora Ephron's classic vinaigrette dressing, steamed broccoli with lemon butter sauce, and some kind of cold nosh like stuffed celery or an olive and cheese platter.

If I have the time, I might also make some kind of casserole side dish. I'm part Greek, so I'd like to make a pastichio (a Greek lasagna) without meat or buy a frozen pack of cheese or spinach pies (about $10 for 12). This is quite inexpensive and definitely rounds out a meal.

If you have some guests who don't eat meat or he just don't like pork or lamb. Homemade hummus and guacamole are great appetizers, and both are easy and fairly inexpensive to make. Sometimes I serve cheese or spinach pies as appetizers and later, bring the leftovers to the table when dinner is served. When I'm trying to impress, I'll make stuffed mushrooms, which are relatively inexpensive ($1.99 for the mushrooms, plus breadcrumbs, Parmesan cheese and butter), but fairly time-consuming to prepare. I might also dress up deviled eggs with a topping of caviar or smoked bacon bits.

Dessert, which I make the night before the party, is usually a pie, with vanilla ice cream, or homemade whipped cream. I find pies incredibly easy to make, and they are always well received. If you prefer not to make your own crust frozen pie crust works just fine (especially the crust at Aldi's). Occasionally I make walnut brownies (from a mix), or cookies.

I always put a pitcher of cold water on the dinner table, so I set my table with two glasses—one for water, one for something else. I always buy 2 L bottles of cola, a caffeine-free soda, and a diet soda, so I have a variety of drinks to offer my guests. I only buy name brands, which I can often get for a 3 for $5 deal, because I don't want to announce to my guests that I'm a cheapskate. Besides, I find on these items I really often *can* taste the difference and so, I imagine, would my guests.

For alcoholic beverages, I usually just offer wine or beer with a sit-down dinner. If I am having a buffet, I will often put out a pitcher of a mixed drink, such as margaritas or martinis in the summer. I also make a mean champagne punch!

I only serve wine and beer that I would drink myself. When I see a bottle of wine on sale at the local wholesale store or liquor store, I will try it myself and see how it holds up. This way I can usually offer my guests a good Merlot (Papi), white Zinfandel (Berringer's for turkey) or Pinot Grigio for about $10 a bottle (the wholesale clubs will sell 2 litter bottles). For beer, I try to find a 12 pack or a good national brand for between $13 and $20.

If I know that a number of guests are non-drinkers, I may buy three pack of sparkling apple cider, which I have found for about $7 at my local wholesale club. However, they only seem to stock this around Thanksgiving, Christmas and Easter. White and red grape juice (about $5 for a 64 ounce bottle or can) also works well for non-drinkers, and you could spruce it up by making it a spritzer (half seltzer, half juice).

In the summer, I'd like to offer my guests champagne punch, or sangria, which they all seem to love and fits easily into any party budget. However, this just doesn't seem to work on cold winter nights. I might also offer homemade lemonade, or iced tea instead of soft drinks in warmer weather.

I always offer my guests coffee or tea after dinner. I keep a small jar of instant, decaffeinated coffee on hand, in case one of my guests just can't take caffeine at night (there was a time when all my friends were pregnant). You can also buy a small portion of decaf and brew it, since most people prefer fresh-brewed to instant. I also keep real cream in the house for company (usually to use for the whipped cream for dessert), which is a nice touch. Of course I offer 2% milk as well. And if I know that my guests are lactose intolerant, I will buy oat or almond milk or Lactaid.

Once you've planned the menu, you have to plan the shopping. I get whatever I can—the meat, beverages, some vegetables (potatoes, apples for pie), and any frozen foods—way ahead of time, usually when I do my weekly shopping. Anything I have to get fresh, such as cream and salad fixings, I buy the morning of the party, after reviewing my menu the night before.

Setting the Table

Part of setting the table is planning the layout of the food and the flow of guests. Once you know how many people are coming, you know whether you are having a sit down dinner or buffet.

I usually have two stacked tables on either side of the main couch, where I place my appetizers. If you have a coffee table, this is a good location for your hors d'oeuvres as well.

If I am having the full number of guests I can accommodate for dinner (which is 16 for my table), I will also put a stack table near the dining table for extra beverages and ice (so I don't have to get up 10 times) and perhaps the salad, after everyone has been served (this leaves more space on the table).

If you don't have stack tables, don't go out and buy them. Unless you live in the wilderness, you can certainly borrow them from a neighbor. People over 50 believed religiously in stack tables, so if you have friends of this generation (or parents or in-laws nearby), you're probably in luck. If you find them very useful, after borrowing a set a couple of times, you can usually find them at garage sales.

I believe quite strongly in using some kind of tablecloth, and also in coasters and trivets, but that's only because I finally have some nice (new) furniture, and I am not partial to watermarks and stains, no matter how charming or interesting their provenance.

Flea markets are great places to look for it-could-have-been-in-my-family lace heirlooms at a fraction of the price you would pay for them if they were new. And don't skip those famous January white sales when department stores will reduce everything just to get you back in the stores after Christmas.

If you are using more than one table, the color of your tablecloths should match, unless the holiday you're celebrating is a two toner (red and green for Christmas, black and orange for Halloween). However, they do not have to be the same pattern or material. You can mix lace and cloth, as long as they are the same color.

Gold is a good color for tablecloths. It's rich and elegant and usually available during the white sales because people tend to go for the basics. If you have a favorite color that goes with the décor of your home, you might want to buy two or three tablecloths in that shade when they're on sale.

Coasters usually come in sets of four, so for a party of 16 you can't be expected to have them match. However, if you entertain a lot, you might want to invest in four matching sets of silver-plated coasters. You should be able to pick up a set any time of the year at a discount store, and you might just be able to get a set for cheap right after Christmas. You can also borrow them from friends if you're having a fairly fancy gathering—everyone you know probably has at least one set of these coasters.

No one expects your trivets or hot plates to match, but it's a nice touch if they do. Again, if you can pick up the silver plated ones when you find them on sale, buy three or four matching ones when you see them at a good price, you're way ahead of the game.

I like to have a centerpiece on my table, whether or not I am celebrating an occasion. Sometimes I just put together an assortment of candlesticks, which should match in both material (glass, silver, or brass—you can pick most of these up at a dollar store or flea market), and candle color (white and gold are good here, too) or flowers (fresh or silk is fine), or a basket of fruit or bread.

If you're artistic, try making a centerpiece. There are many ideas and kits available at craft stores and through Internet searches. While I prefer store-bought or craft fair purchases, I did make one centerpiece that would work for any table anytime of the year.

Take a plain glass vase (the kind you usually get with a flower delivery), paint a simple floral design on it with acrylic paint, and tie a ribbon (try gold, pink or lavender) around the neck. It really dresses up your table. If you're like me, and keep every vase you've ever received, this is an opportunity to finally make good use out of something everyone else thinks you should throw away. If not, you can pick up a vase at a yard sale or thrift shop or even buy one from the local florist for very little.

Cloth napkins are nice, but they're an extravagance, especially if they're white. If you're serving red wine or any kind of red sauce, or one of your guests wears the new lipstick that promises never to come off (except on your napkins), you're safer with paper. I recommend fancy white paper table napkins (Vanity Fair is the brand that comes to mind, usually a pack of 40 for around $3), which you can get at a dollar store or in lots of 300 at a wholesale club. You might also want to buy a package of cocktail napkins to serve with drinks and appetizers. Fortunately, these are still readily available at dollar stores and have not gone up in price in years (and come in almost any color you can imagine).

Your dishes, glasses, and utensils should match. By this, I mean, you should try to have dishes with the same color and pattern. If you don't have service for 16 (and can't borrow it), your best bet would be to use two complete sets of eight and alternate them at the table. If you are serving 12, but only have service for eight and have to borrow dishes or use two different sets, you should set the table with six of each pattern. Same goes for the flatware and glassware.

For utensils, you should never mix silver and stainless steel. Borrow one set of either to make sure that all your flatware matches.

Make sure you have the right number of pieces (don't forget salad forks, and coffee spoons). You don't want to have to run back into the kitchen to wash all the forks and spoons for dessert. Don't forget the serving utensils (salad servers, large spoons for the mashed potatoes, gravy, spoon, pie server, ladle).

Glasses should also match, and you shouldn't mix crystal and glass, if you can help it. Not only should the material of the glasses match, but the type should match as well (wine glasses, water glasses, etc.). However, the pattern or design can be different, if it's not too obvious, or if their difference is the point.

I find that sets of glasses (usually 12 to a box with four water, four rocks and four juice glasses) are sold in every discount store and are very cheap. You should be able to pick up a number of boxes for under $25, especially at places like IKEA, Bed Bath & Beyond, Target and Walmart. I've seen boxed sets on sale for as little as $5 at discount stores. For mousse-like desserts, berries with cream, or cold soups, you might want to consider balloon glasses which you can certainly pick up at the dollar store or flea market.

You will also need to make sure you have the right serving pieces for your company, such as platters, bread baskets, coffee pot, sugar, creamer, and salt and pepper shakers. All these items should match—that is, they should be all silver or all china. What you don't have, you should be able to borrow from friends or neighbors—they probably received a lot of these items as wedding presents. If you borrow silver, part of the payback might be that you polish it, since the owners probably haven't used it since the day they got it.

You may also have to borrow a second coffee maker, which is preferable to serving only 12 cups of coffee at a time and making some of your guests wait for the second serving.

If you're serving to a roast, you might even have to "borrow" a neighbor's oven or microwave. I once made Thanksgiving dinner for 16 and had to use my downstairs neighbor's oven for the appetizers and dessert (that was before I learned to make the dessert the night before). And I did invite that neighbor to dinner.

When having a sit-down dinner, you should never use paper or plastic plates and flatware. If you feel the need to use them, then you should be having a buffet.

I hate running back-and-forth to the kitchen once my guests arrive, so I try very hard to have as much as possible done ahead of time. That's why I set up the stack tables with appetizers and it's why I set the table before the guests arrive. If you have children, teaching them to set the table for both company and the nightly family dinner is one of the first skills they should learn.

Last-Minute Preparations

Make your salad about a half an hour before the company is due and put it in the refrigerator, but do not dress it (do make the dressing ahead of time, though). If I'm serving a plate of pickles, olives, and cheese, I prepare the dish early, cover it with plastic wrap, and put it in the fridge. Cold hors d'oeuvres (dips, guacamole, or hummus) should be prepared right before the guests are due, so that they are fresh. If appetizers need to be baked or zapped, I have them ready to go directly into the oven or microwave so that they're hot when my guests arrive as well.

Atmosphere

I'm not a big fan of perfumed candles, aromatherapy, or incense. I believe the smell of a meal cooking, or the aroma of a pie baking is more than enough to enthrall my guests. However, I feel that music is extremely important to setting the mood of the meal. Therefore, I think it's imperative that you set aside some time during the planning stage to decide about how long the party should be (usually four hours for a dinner party) and choose the music you wish to play for your company. Take a few minutes before your guests arrive to make sure the music you've chosen is cued up, or you can choose a channel on Spotify that plays Spanish guitar or smooth jazz.

Whether it's a sit down dinner, party, or buffet, the music should be background music, although it can be a little livelier if you are having a cocktail party. The music you play for your guests should have a uniformity to it—by this I mean, you should not be mixing rock with country and classical.

Since I like my parties to have a theme, I like the music to fit the theme in some way. If I'm having a Christmas dinner, I'll play Christmas music. If the meal is of a certain cuisine, I might play music from that region. If I'm throwing a 30th or 40th birthday party, I might play music from the birthday guest's teenage years. You might choose to just play music from a certain decade, or a certain type (rock, jazz, classical).

Buffets

Most of the rules of sit-down dining apply for buffet style at-home dining, except that you can use paper or plastic plates, flatware, and even tablecloths (which you should buy at a wholesale club, or a discount or dollar store, where you might be able to pick up a pattern of some sort). Everyone understands that you were using too many dishes for the average dishwasher.

A nice touch when having a buffet is to wrap the cutlery in the napkins and tie them with a ribbon, preferably one that goes with the décor. Place them, standing up, in a basket, so that guests can just grab a setting without having to fumble for the individual pieces.

You might want to think about putting an extra wastebasket near the dining table so that people don't have to crowd into the kitchen to throw away their dirty dishes. If you live in a state that recycles, you might want to have a separate wastebasket just for cans and bottles. This will also make it easier for people to clean up after themselves, and you won't have so many empty bottles to collect after the party.

When setting the table, make sure you put out an ample number of napkins, as people will inevitably spill things, and you want them to be able to clean up as fast as possible. If there is more than one course being served (appetizers, main course, dessert) you should have at least the number of courses times the number of guests and napkins (3 courses x 25 guests = 75 napkins). The same math applies for cups because people tend to throw out empty cups and then get fresh ones when they they're thirsty again.

If you are using more than one table, you should have the same items on each table, so people won't crowd around the turkey and skip the salad. Furthermore, at large gatherings, having an extra table, help spread people out and keeps the buffet line moving.

For beverages, put a punch bowl on the table or put a cooler full of ice with beer and soda in it under the table. You can also place an ice bucket on the table and display the wine, beer, and soda on one side of the table. Make sure you leave at least two bottle openers on the table if the beer or wine require them. Always put out a pitcher of cold water for your guests too.

The food you decide to serve will depend on the number of guests you have and perhaps on the time of year (lighter food in the summer). For 25 people and under, I might serve a large turkey or roast and a casserole (lasagna, ham and spaghetti casserole). If I'm having more than 25, I would serve several main courses (Greek meatballs, which I can make the night before; a casserole, which I will make ahead and reheat before the party; and a roast), as well as a number of side dishes. Pasta dishes are also great for large crowds.

If you are serving a roast, you will probably need two gravy boats, and at least two sets of salt and pepper shakers.

Keep in mind, too, that finger food is the easiest thing for standing guests to eat. Gravies and sauces are likely to end up on your floor and upholstery if your guests have nowhere to sit.

Desert can be much the same as what you would serve as a sit-down dinner, although I would probably make two to three different pies (apple, blueberry, strawberry, or banana cream), or brownies. For a buffet, homemade cookies are also a great choice.

Unless you can get your local church or PTA to lend you their coffee maker, you are definitely going to have to borrow a second coffee machine. You should have at least two creamers and sugar bowls as well.

Many couples receive large hot plates, crockpots, and silver warming trays as wedding presents, so you should be able to borrow as many of these as you need from friends and family. Just make sure you don't wait until the last minute to locate these important appliances. (Sometimes your friends think they know where things are, and then realize the night of your party that they threw them out.) You might want to look into borrowing stack tables to place strategically around the room as well.

Cocktail Parties

A cocktail party is any party where dinner is not served. I gave a lot of cocktail parties and was invited to a lot of them when I was younger, single, and childless.

Cocktail parties start later than dinner parties, and usually end later too. During my parents' time, they used to start early and end early so people could go out to dinner afterwards, but today they tend to be after dinner gatherings.

Some cocktail party invitations give a specific time, such as 6:00 to 8:00 p.m. This means that the party is finite, usually because there is another event to attend, such as a live performance. If the invitation just states a time to begin, such as 7:00 p.m., then the party is open ended. I like to start a cocktail party between 7:00 and 8:00 p.m. and hope that the last guest will be on their way home no later than midnight, but that's really up to you and your guests (and perhaps your neighbors).

Even though you're not required to feed your guests, I always have enough appetizers and finger foods available for someone to make a meal of it, if they have to. I'm always worried that someone will have too much to drink on an empty stomach and drive home.

For the average cocktail party, my appetizers include lots of chips and dips. I offer homemade salsa and bowls of taco chips, as well as guacamole. Near the bowls of pretzels and potato chips (staples at this kind of thing), I place small bowls of dip. I make popcorn on the stove (I read about carcinogens in microwave popcorn and just do it the old-fashioned way, which I do think tastes better) and dribble on a little melted butter. I put out little bowls of M&Ms, chocolate kisses, and Reese's peanut butter cups which disappear immediately. I have also found that people love to be offered bowls of nuts, especially something more exotic than peanuts or mixed nuts, so I often put out a few helpings of shelled nuts, like sugar roasted almonds or pistachios. All of this, while being pretty effortless, adds up to a nice variety of nibbles.

The above items can be bought quite cheaply in bulk at your local wholesale club. The candy might even be less expensive at your supermarket, if you manage to shop right after a holiday.

For a slightly fancier party, I would also include an assortment of cheeses, with crackers and French bread wedges. I might also offer an assortment of salamis slices.

If you choose to serve hot appetizers, you can buy packages of 36 of almost anything at your local wholesale club. This usually includes such hors d'oeuvres as miniature hotdogs, cheese puffs, eggrolls, and poppers. Most of these wholesale clubs offer shoppers a sample of this kind of fare various times throughout the year, so you should have a pretty good idea of how these frozen foods will taste. My one rule of thumb with these appetizers is never offer something to your guests you haven't tried yourself.

In addition to the store-bought appetizers, I might offer one or two homemade items, such as Greek meatballs, (which can be served hot or cold) or my reliable hummus, with pita bread slices.

You might also add a fruit platter, with grapes and apple and pear slices. In the summer, you might try offering an assortment of strawberries, raspberries, and blueberries with whipped cream. I've been to parties where creative hostesses have carved out a watermelon and filled the rind with melon balls and assorted summer fruit. Fresh pineapple chunks are also well received in the summer.

On the beverages front, I would do much the same as a sit-down dinner or buffet party regarding soda, wine, and beer. However, if my cocktail party has a theme (disco, New Year's Eve, bon voyage), I might make a pitcher or two or three of a mixed drink that I felt would go well with the scene, such as tequila sunrise, or champagne punch, or piña coladas, all of which are much cheaper to make if you buy the ingredients in large quantities. Just make sure you have a lot of ice and enough to go around for at least three drinks per guest. You might want to borrow an extra blender if you're throwing a frozen drinks party.

Setting up a cocktail party is much like setting up a buffet. You place everything on the dining room table, with snack bowls spread strategically throughout your home, as well as the extra wastebaskets. If it's a casual cocktail party (end of the semester, office party), you could use plastic and paper. If it's black tie (10th wedding anniversary), you need to go to cloth and silver, but you can use those plastic champagne glasses.

Music is especially important at cocktail parties. If you're having a party, where you expect to talk to one another, you need to have four or five hours of seamless background music picked out.

If you're having a party where you expect your guests to dance, or at least get up and wiggle, you need to plan the music carefully. You might also have to move your living room furniture out of the way. Anything that can break probably will, and your guests will feel less inhibited if you give them the space they need.

A cocktail party is the one kind of party where I've had to tell guests it's time to go home. Most sit-down or buffet parties break up after one or two couples leave. Changing the tone of the music to something soft when you think it's time to wind down is one subtle way of calling it a night. Some people play certain songs to indicate the night is over like "Closing Time" by Semisonic, "Hit the Road Jack" by Ray Charles, or "Last Dance" by Donna Summer.

People also start to get the hint if you start cleaning up aggressively (folding up the tablecloths, bringing the snack bowls in to the kitchen). However, if none of the above works, don't be ashamed to say the party's over by offering the last few guests their coats. Part of the whole idea of throwing parties is for you to enjoy your company, and for you to want to do it again. Don't let one rude guest lead you to second thoughts.

Sample Menus

Below are sample menus and estimated costs for three parties: a sit-down dinner, a buffet party, and a cocktail party. Cost estimates are based on average prices in the eastern United States supermarkets or wholesale clubs. This should give you an idea of the kind of budgeting your party will require.

Sit-Down Dinner for Twelve

Home-made Hummus dip with pita bread $10.00

1 16 oz can of chick peas
Juice of one lemon
Tahini paste
Pita Bread

You will be able to use the Tahini paste multiple times, so this is actually economical if you entertain a lot.
Of course, you can just buy a pre-made humous dip and Pita bread, which should run between $6 or $7 total.

Guacamole $4.00

2 ripe Haas avocados
Lemon juice
2 tablespoons chili powder
Crushed garlic clove

Roast turkey $9.66

14 lb. turkey @ $.69 a lb
(you might get this cheaper during holiday Season – in 2026, I was able to buy turkey at $.39 a lb. at my local supermarket)

Lori Perkins

Mashed Potatoes $2.99

5 lb. bag of Idaho or similar potatoes
3 tablespoons, butter
¼ cup cream or milk or half and half
(I assume you have the butter and milk on hand).

Homemade Cornbread Stuffing $0.99

8 ½ box of Jiffy cornbread mix
some raisins
10 to 15 walnuts broken into pieces
sliced bell pepper
chopped onions
2 tablespoons butter
(again, assuming you have raisins and walnuts on hand, as well as onions)

Salad $7.50

2 heads of green or red leaf lettuce
3 plum or on-the-vine tomatoes
Onion
a few olives
walnuts if desired
oil and vinegar
(maybe some of the pepper strips from the cornbread above)

Glazed Carrots $1.99

6 oz. bag of baby carrots
2 tablespoons sugar
2 tablespoons butter

Apple pie $9.00

6 or 7 apples (bag)
pie crust
½ cup sugar
½ cup flour

Chocolate cream pie $4.00

1 box chocolate pudding mix

5 or 6 graham crackers
2 tablespoons melted butter

Whipped cream $4.00
1 pint heavy whipping cream
sugar to taste

Soda $6.00
3 2 L bottles

Wine $30.00
3 bottles
(I can get wine for less in NYC, but I am being generous here)

Total **$87.13**

There will be tax on the wine. In some states, your food will be taxed as well.

When I wrote the first edition of this book in 1999, this party cost $47.45.

You can reduce the cost of the meal by making less expensive appetizers, or serving a punch and iced tea instead of soda or wine. You can also reduce the cost of the party by finding less expensive wine. For instance, in New York city, I can buy a 1 1/2 L bottle of Papi wine for $11.99.

When I calculate the cost of the meal, I am not counting the cost of basic staples such a sugar, butter, flour, coffee, or tea that would be used in small quantities. The meal could run you as much as $25 more if you have to buy everything from scratch.

Buffet for 35

Hummus $9.00
(cost goes up about $1.00 every 10 extra people you serve).

Guacamole $6.00
(Cost goes up an additional $1 for every extra 10 people)

Lori Perkins

Potato Chips 2 party size bags (at wholesale club)	$9.00
Tortilla Chips Party size bag	$5.00
Onion Dip with Blue Cheese 1 pint sour cream 1 package instant onion soup mix ½ lb. crumbled blue cheese	$5.99
Roast turkey	$9.66
Lasagna (2 trays homemade) 1 lb. boxes of lasagna noodles 1 lb. ground beef, ricotta cheese mozzarella cheese, marinara sauce	$24.00
Salad Twice as much as previous party	$15.00
Stuffed celery I stalk celery cream cheese crumbled blue cheese (use leftovers from dip above) paprika for garnish	$5.00
Cornbread stuffing (twice as much as the dinner party)	$4.00
Apple Pie	$9.00
Walnut Brownies (mix)	$4.00
Oatmeal cookies with raisins and walnuts	$5.00
Whipped Cream	$4.00

Soda, $10.00
5 2 L bottles

White wine $20.00
2 bottles

Red wine $20.00
2 bottles

Case of beer $30.00
(You can buy a 30 pack of some of the cheaper beers, or a 24 pack of better brands)

Ice (5 lbs.) $5.00

2 paper or plastic tablecloths $2.50
(go to a dollar store, where they may cost $1.25 each now)

Chinet plates $8.00

Dinner napkins $3.00

Plastic utensils $6.00
(you can get these at the dollar store or order from Temu)

Plastic tumblers $5.00

Total **$224.15**

Again, the cost of the party can be greatly reduced if you offer iced tea and lemonade instead of soda, and serve a punch or eliminate the alcoholic beverages. However, even with alcohol this party comes to less than $7 per person, which is very good. Leave out the alcohol lowers the cost to about $5 per person.

The cost of this party in 1999 was around $117.

Fancy Cocktail Party for 50

Hummus $11.00
(cost goes up about $1.00 every 10 extra people you serve).

Guacamole $8.00
(Cost goes up an additional $1 for every extra 10 people)

Potato Chips $14.00
3 party size bags (at wholesale club)

Tortilla Chips $10.00
Party size bag

Onion Dip with Blue Cheese $12.00
2 pint sour cream
2 package instant onion soup mix
½ lb. crumbled blue cheese

Salsa (homemade or store bought) $8.00

Pretzels Large bag $5.00

Candy (assorted- M & M's, Lindt truffles, kisses, etc.) $6.00

Cheese (assorted – brie, cheddar, Saga bleu, Allouette) $15.00

Bread $6.00
2 loaves if Italian or French bread cut in slices

Carrs crackers, $10.00
4 boxes from wholesale store

Olives, Assorted – Spanish, Greek, black $10.00

Greek meatballs $25.00
5 lbs. of beef makes about 60 meatballs (buy the tube of ground beef at Aldi's or Costco)

Pasta Salad 3 lbs. macaroni with dressing and peas and ham	$10.00
Soda, 9 bottles assorted, including seltzer	$18.00
Beer, 2 cases	$60.00
Wine 3 1/1/2 litter bottles	$45.00
Ice, plates, etc. about the same as above for buffet party	$35.00
Carrot cake or sheet cake for 50	$30.00
Total	**$338.00**

Once again, you can reduce the cost of the party by making a punch and iced tea and lemonade. You may want to try sangria or pitchers of drinks for this kind of party, instead of the beer and wine, which accounts for about a third of the party cost. You could also replace the Greek meatballs and pasta salad with store-bought, ready-made hors d'oeuvres (which should be about 150 individual pieces), if you don't have the time or desire to make everything.

This party comes to a little under $7 a head, which is still a good deal. Aside from cutting back on the alcohol, you could lower the price per person by making your own dessert, or cutting out some of the food. And there's a lot of food here!

In 1999, this party ran about $185.

Chapter Four: Catered Parties

If you are having more than 60 people, or if you just don't want to do all the cleaning, shopping, schlepping, and setting up yourself, you might want to consider having your party catered.

Catering might sound expensive, but there are many different ways to do it. It all depends on what you want and what you can afford. However, catering will always cost more than doing everything yourself.

The three basic categories of catering are: in your home, in rented space, or in a restaurant. Of course, the more you have someone else do for you (such as setting up and cleaning up), the more expensive it will be.

Catering in Your Home

The first catered party I had was my parents 25th wedding anniversary (I was 24). My aunt knew a woman in her neighborhood who supplemented her Social Security checks by cooking and baking from home, so we were able to get a good price on homemade food. This is actually a wonderful way to cater a party, if you know someone who is a good cook, and might like to earn some extra money. This is an especially good idea if you are looking for a particular ethnic favorite. Someone who has been making a specialty for years will do a much better job than the generic caterer.

You can inquire at your local house of worship if there is a member of the congregation who might be interested in making extra money this way. It doesn't even have to be your church or synagogue. You can just call the parish house and ask to speak with the secretary. They usually know everything and everybody. Some of the retired older women might be quite interested in baking you a cake, and making a lasagna or two. If there is a senior center near you, you might call there as well. Check the classified ads in the local newspaper as well or try posting an inquiry on your neighborhood Next-Door app or local Facebook group.

We catered the hot food and the dessert, which was a black forest cake (something I would never attempt from scratch), and the rest we did ourselves, which included the family favorites. For drinks we served only my parents' two favorite alcoholic beverages—champagne cocktails for my mom and Manhattans for my dad—on trays in plastic champagne glasses or drink glasses, and that was a big hit.

There were 35 people and the party came to about $100, which was a lot of money for me at that time (this was about 40 years ago). However, I could never have afforded to take these people to a restaurant on my meager salary, and they all had a fairly luxurious evening without breaking my bank account. A party like this would run me at least $500 today.

I have since had many a catered party in my home (or a borrowed home) from the assorted cold cut platter and sheet cake set-up to the shrimp cocktail and lasagna/meatballs/chicken dish affair. As with all parties, the first thing to do is to set a budget and see what you can get for the price. You have to decide which is more important or where your flexibility is—time or money.

For me, if I've decided to have some of the party catered, it's because I know I don't have the time to get everything ready myself. However, there is some mystical point of being overcharged where I will decide I'll get up at 6:00 in the morning and do it myself rather than get ripped off. Only *you* know where that point is.

If you are going for the dip and veggies platter, assorted cold cuts and sheet cake party, I strongly recommend that you order everything from your local wholesale club (call ahead of time). It will be much cheaper than the supermarket deli or local caterer. It will also be almost as cheap as buying everything in bulk and setting it up yourself. The one drawback is that you (or a family member, or someone who loves you very much) will have to pick up everything the day of the party, unless you splurge on Instacart, which is certainly worth it for something like this.

The other advantage to this is that you, not the caterer, get to decide how much food you need. Every party I've ever had done by a catering business, left me with so much extra food that I had to force it into the hands of departing guests. In one instance, I gave pounds of leftover cold cuts to a homeless shelter. If you can see the food ahead of time, you'll have a much better idea of how many people a platter will feed.

For the average affair of crudites with dip, cold cuts, and a sheet cake, you should expect a wholesale club cold cut platter to feed 20 people ($30 each) and each veggie and dip platter to feed 20 ($30.00 each). The sheet cake will run $50 to feed 60, so the basic cost of this kind of party is around $5.00 per person, without drinks, and any extras you might want to throw in (like a tub of hummus, a salad, shrimp cocktail).

If you hire a caterer, remember the caterer always errs on the side of abundance, so if you say you need food for 50 people expect enough food to feed at least 60. If you're having 50 people tell the caterer 40. You'll still have more than enough food.

Always comparison shop with caterers. I do this over the phone and ask them to email me their menus and prices. There can be tremendous price discrepancies. If you like one place much better than the other, but the other is a lot cheaper, you can always quote the others' price to try to get the one you like to meet it. Most caterers will. They don't want to lose the business.

New York City caterers (which are the ones I deal with) charge between $10 and $15 per person for a cold cut platter (with an assortment of bread) and veggies with dip. The sheet cake is extra (about $1.50 per person), although the classier the establishment, the fancier the cake selection. Most caterers give you plates, utensils, and napkins with your order.

However, the caterer will also charge you tax, which could be a substantial amount, and you have to tip the guys who deliver the food to you. Sometimes (especially in New-York) they even charge you for the delivery.

You can always negotiate with the caterer. You can keep the cost of the cold cuts down by limiting your selection, to, say, turkey, and roast beef with American and provolone cheese. (*Hint*: always order smoked turkey; it stays fresh longer than baked turkey, so you can eat it longer if you over order). You should always tell the caterer the price is a little more than you expected, even if it's not, and ask how you can keep the price down.

The giant hero sandwich (in either the Italian or classic combination) is also a good way to cater a party and keep the cost down. These run between $20 and $30 for three feet, which feeds somewhere between 10 and 20 people, and are usually supplemented by vats of coleslaw, potato salad, macaroni salad, or even a regular salad. I tend to order these from my local wholesale store.

It is a little more expensive to cater hot food for your guests. The lasagna/meatballs/ chicken dish set up usually runs at least $10 per person. The caterer usually throws in a salad of some sort with this, as well as the plates, utensils, napkins. The chafing dishes and sternos should be included in this price, but some caterers might ask for a refundable deposit on each item.

A more luxurious party could even feature a roast (turkey will run between $50 and $75, depending on the size) or fancier meals like Chicken Parmesan or shrimp scampi, but once you go in that direction, the catering charge per person usually climbs into double digits. To my mind, you might as well go to a restaurant, where they cook it, serve it, and clean it up afterwards. If you're a good negotiator, you can probably find a restaurant that will serve your party for about the same cost as doing this at home.

Renting Space for a Catered Party

If you know you can't or don't want to have the party in your home, there are a number of options, most of which depend on how fancy the party is, and how much money you have to spend.

When I'm faced with these circumstances, my first thoughts are, *Can I borrow someone's house? Is there some space I can use that I don't have to pay for*? I borrowed my aunt's apartment for my parents 25th anniversary, I used my office for my husband's surprise 30th party, and I had a small party for my son's christening at the church where he was baptized. A friend hosted her son's summer birthday party in a local park, where she could use the outdoor picnic tables.

Of course, if you borrow someone else's home, you have to invite them to the party, and you have to offer to give them the lion's share of the leftovers. You also have to offer either your own home in exchange (if it's a good friend's house and they're hosting your spouse's surprise birthday party for you) or you will help when they have a party and need a hand.

You should not ask to "borrow" a home from someone you do not consider a close friend or colleague (if you borrow the office). You also have to be responsible for all cleaning up and you have to replace anything that gets ruined or broken. If the rug gets badly stained, you have to be willing to pay for it to be cleaned. In some ways, it's just easier to rent space.

The most likely rental spaces are church rec rooms and party rooms in apartment buildings co-ops. Social organizations such as the local Y, the Kiwanis club, veterans organizations, the American Legion, and some municipal buildings in small towns also rent space. Check local listings under caterers, as well as the local paper and post queries on your local Next-Door app.

Most of these facilities have a kitchen off of the main room, where you can store items in the refrigerator or heat things up in the oven or microwave. They also usually have extra tables and chairs and coat racks for you to use in setting up your party (these items are pricey to rent if your space doesn't provide them). Sometimes they even have a dance floor.

Renting a rec room or party room usually runs between $100 and $500, and you might be asked to write an additional check for a refundable security deposit (in case anything is damaged).

I held a memorial service for my mother in the church where she was once a member, and I had to rent the space for $1000, as well as purchase additional insurance for the event. There were at least 100 people and we served food afterwards.

Every space you rent will have its own set of rules and regulations. Most churches do not allow you to serve alcohol on the premises. Some places don't want you to play loud music. Some buildings only stay open until a certain time.

If you decide to use rented space, you have to be very careful in planning your affair. Don't assume that you can set up the party the night before (if you're having a luncheon) because the space may be in use then. If you store your nonperishables (plates and soda) in the kitchen before the party, there's always the possibility that someone might not know whose stuff it is, and some, or all, of it may be missing when you show up to set up for your party (if you do store stuff the night before, put tags on it with your event described such as "Perkins Party 1/1/202"). This also applies to leaving leftovers in the refrigerator until the next day after the party: they might not be there when you return.

Almost any building or institution in a major city can be rented for the right price for a private party. I know a couple who rented out the Central Park Zoo for their child's first birthday. (It ran them about $6000 in the year 1999). Old homes that have been turned into museums are often used for this purpose. Most of these sites are quite expensive to rent, but they are sometimes free or rented at cost to an employee. If you work for a private university, they usually have property that you might be able to rent for a fraction of what they would charge an outsider. Professional clubs (alumni, sports, work-related), often also have a wonderful space that they make available to members.

If you are renting space, and having the food delivered by a separate caterer, the caterer will not set it up for you unless you negotiate this. You'll have to negotiate a time to go to the premises and arrange where the food and beverages will be placed. I would recommend you do this an hour or so before the party, especially if you're planning to prepare some of the food yourself right before the party, such as a punch.

If the party is for a special occasion, and you have decorations and balloons, you'll have to put those up yourself before the party. Make sure the hall shows you where the ladder is. Expect to bring your own staple gun and scotch tape. Don't forget aluminum foil and plastic bags or Tupperware for leftovers.

Hosting Your Party in a Restaurant

Throwing a party in a restaurant is the most expensive way to entertain, but it's also the least amount of work—no setting up, no serving, no cleaning up.

Just because you've decided to take the path of least exertion, doesn't mean you have to blindly hand over your credit card. Everything can be negotiated, even if you're having a wedding reception at the Waldorf Astoria (*especially* if you're having a wedding reception at the Waldorf!).

If I am going to have my party in a restaurant, I want the intimacy of serving in my home with the comfort of not having to cook and serve, so I look for a place that has a private room or section for my party, whether it's for 12 or 35. Otherwise, you might as well have a few friends meet in the restaurant while people you don't know ogle your birthday cake and presents (I have been to parties like this, and they're a little too casual for my taste).

Friday and Saturday nights are premium evenings, so if you can schedule your party on a Sunday or a weeknight, you should be able to save money. Most restaurants will charge less if you fill the place on Monday night than if you take up the back room on the busiest nights.

If you do have some date and time flexibility, try having a luncheon, brunch, or even breakfast, instead of dinner. The earlier the meal, the cheaper the price. If the restaurant offers an early bird special to its regular customers, you can ask if they will give you an early bird special price for your group affair. Also, people are less inclined to drink alcohol earlier in the day, so there's usually a savings in that area as well.

Different types of meals are also priced differently in most restaurants. The chicken and pasta meals are the least expensive, followed by fish, and then beef. If you are having children attend the meal, it is important that the restaurant of your choice have a children's menu with the reduced prices that most children's menus feature.

You'll have to be comfortable with asking for ways to reduce the price of the meal per person, and you will have to do it many times to get the best price ("What if I have the party another night?" "What if I only offered chicken and pasta dishes?" "Do you have a children's menu?"). If you don't ask, the restaurant will most likely not offer the information.

Of course, you can keep the cost of the meal down by not offering appetizers or just offering you guests the house salad with the meal. The restaurant might offer pitchers of soda and ice tea instead of individual glasses, if you ask.

Another way to keep costs down is to bring your own wine or champagne. Be prepared to be charged a corking fee, which is still substantially less than what you might have to pay if the restaurant supplied the wine. If you are going to offer more of a liquor selection, you could ask for a price on pitchers of margaritas, Bloody Mary's, mimosas, and beer.

If you want something really special for dessert, or a family member makes a special treat, you might consider bringing your own dessert, which will certainly cost less than the restaurant's dessert menu. You can also threaten to bring in your own dessert, which might make the restaurant give you a break on this feature of the meal.

Remember that on top of the price per meal, you will have to pay tax at and a gratuity, which is often at least 18%, and after Covid more likely to be 20%.

Having an affair catered is supposed to make your life easier so that you can more fully enjoy the company of your guests and the special event that has brought you all together.

Chapter Five: Special Occasion Parties

Most of the parties I throw are for special occasions, such as birthdays and holidays. Most people have a basic party concept they follow that they know how to do well, and that they can dress up for that special occasion. However, it is the details of each gathering, even if you have the same people for the same reasons every year, that will make each party stand out.

I know that I will throw at least 25 gatherings or parties a year (birthday parties, Thanksgiving, a number of Christmas get-togethers, an office party, Easter, New Year's, summer barbecues, as well as sit-down dinners for friends and family), so I am always on the lookout for decorations that will enhance the gathering at various times of the year.

I have a large box of Christmas stuff that includes the usual bulbs and nativity, but also includes tablecloths, a set of Christmas dishes, platters, and a ceramic Santa cookie jar, which I often use as a centerpiece. When my family and friends come for the annual holiday gatherings, my house is totally decked out in Christmas décor. Most of the stuff I've picked up for half price or better the day after Christmas (all major department stores have an after Christmas sale), or at a dollar store or discount shop. I once bought a 10-piece Dickens porcelain village for $5 over Labor Day, and it's now one of our family heirlooms.

I've done the same thing for Halloween, which is a big deal in our home (my son called me the queen of Halloween when he was young). We have another box in storage that is bursting with Halloween tablecloths, salt and pepper shakers, potholders, and decorative table centerpieces. Did you know that Halloween is the second most popular commercial holiday in America?

I also have a lot of nice things for Thanksgiving and Easter, since I'm the one who always hosts these holidays, although many of those accessories are more generically seasonal (fall or spring), so I can use them for a longer period of time. It's wonderful to know I don't have to go searching for tablecloths and centerpieces the day before the holiday.]

I have a neighbor who is the favorite aunt to a number of children of all ages. She often finds herself throwing a makeshift party for a group of 10 to 12 kids, and she is always prepared. Always have a fresh supply of birthday candles on hand, which you can buy for a dollar a box. Many of the holiday centerpieces I picked up over the years are ceramic and you might find (or make) one that has a birthday motif. The same goes for a tablecloth.

However, there are some parties that call for unique and creative approaches, such as showers and retirement bashes. These occasions come so rarely in our lives, that we really want to make them as special as possible, without going broke.

Baby and Bridal Showers

No woman alive has escaped forced attendance at showers, many of which are so uninspired they can scarcely be called parties. Some of these showers have also been amazingly expensive, just because the person throwing it was too lazy to do anything creative. But baby and bridal showers are two kinds of parties where you can really go overboard with all that cute kitschy stuff, so do it up, if that's your thing!

When I got married, I was running a local newspaper and was in the process of getting sued (for political reasons), so I was not very into the oohs and aahs of being the bride. I told my mother and matron of honor that I didn't want a bridal shower, but I'm glad they didn't listen to me. So this is the first rule here: no matter what the bride says, throw her a shower. If she's really against it, and she's hardly even having a wedding (the old justice of the peace routine at City Hall), throw her an anti-shower (make everyone wear black, get black balloons, spray paint some silk flowers black, etc.), but do *something* to commemorate the event even if it's a third or seventh trip down the aisle (and you've thrown all the other showers), do it one more time.

Remember that the purpose of the shower is to have a great time with friends on the cusp of this new life change, and to a endow the bride or mother-to-be with as much stuff as possible for her new life. Where you have the shower, what you serve, how fancy the invitations are, don't really matter. What the bride or mom gets is the key.

Invitations to showers today are most likely Evites, unless you want to create an invitation that is a momento of sorts (one friend sent magnets as invitations with the date on them, so that people could put them up on the refrigerator and not forget.) I once received a homemade invitation to a baby shower in the shape of a cloth diaper, with a safety pin secured into it. It was precious and memorable.

Remember to include directions because people will be coming from many different places for this gathering. Also, don't forget to put the RSVP email and your phone number as well as the date to respond to on the invitation.

I've always disliked having a list of the home decor colors, or what to get the bride included with my invitation. If you feel you must, just put a discreet link to where the bride is registered or her Amazon wish list, if she has one. Same thing goes for a baby registry.

Most bridal showers are thrown by the maid of honor, or the bridal party, but a beloved aunt or her favorite cousin could take on the task. This usually happens when the wedding party has to come in from out of town. Sometimes, the bride gets two showers this way—one for family and one for friends and coworkers.

My experience is that showers tend to be on weekend afternoons. An office shower is often during lunch or right after work

I've been to extremely fancy showers in expensive restaurants where I hardly knew what silverware to use, and one in which I was asked to bring $10 towards the purchase of the mother-to-be's gift as well as contribute to the potluck luncheon. The latter, by the way, was one of the best showers I've ever been to, because it really made me feel like I was part of an intimate group celebrating something special.

Since showers tend to be in the afternoon, the food is generally lunch or finger food that can double as lunch. That usually means cold cut platters or a big sandwich with an assortment of hot or cold appetizers (lots of veggies and dip) or sandwiches of chicken and tuna salad. Mixed drinks are rarely served (because the mother-to-be can't drink), but a pitcher of margaritas could certainly loosen up any group of celebrants. Most showers feature soft drinks, wine, and perhaps a punch.

Cake is very important to a shower, and you should put some effort into being creative with this menu item, if you can. This can be as simple as asking the store's cake decorator if they have any additional decorations they can put on or draw on. Alternatively, you might consider doing some decorating yourself (interconnecting wedding rings or a stork carrying a baby). You can also go online and see if you can find a cake topper on Etsy or Amazon that works well with your party theme. You can go to a toy, dollar, or party store, and see if you can find some miniature furniture or dolls that you can plant into the icing. If you're truly gifted with cake decorating or are extremely artistic, you might even want to bake your own cake, cut it into an interesting shape (such as a cradle or bells), and decorate it yourself.

There should be an element of fun to the shower, and this can be kicked off by having an open "wishing well" or upside down umbrella full of small gifts for the bride or mother-to-be. Party stores will rent these (the cost is around $50 with an additional security deposit) or you can make your own wishing well out of a laundry basket covered with gift wrapping paper. For my bridal shower, my best friend bought a white wicker hamper, tied a big ribbon around it, and had guests bring an inexpensive household gift, such as dish towels, potholders, and wine openers. I've been to baby showers where we've been asked to do the same thing with guests bringing bottles, pacifiers, and rattles. All of these items can be purchased at the dollar store.

Never feel pressured into overspending for the bigger present. If you're pressed for cash, you can call the mother of the bride or mother-to-be (or the person who's throwing the party), and ask if you can contribute to a bigger present. Often, friends and family members go in together to get some big ticket items such as luggage or strollers. Whatever you gift towards this item should be appreciated.

However, if that doesn't feel right, the other thing you can do is make something (or ask someone you know to make something) for the bride or the baby. Some of my most treasured gifts were the handmade sweaters and booties for my son or the homemade quilts. One older woman from my mother's church made me a collage of my son's birth, which I love (she took a deep frame and glued a miniature crib, birth certificate, etc. into it to create a baby's room). Another woman gave me a sculpture spelling out my son's name in children's alphabet blocks.

If you're a family member and have old wedding pictures from either his or her family or baby pictures, you could have these printed and put together of as a very personal photo album for the bride or new mother.

If you're throwing the shower, or you're part of an important group at the shower, (one of the four aunts, her sorority sisters, etc.) and you're somewhat good at sewing, you could suggest that a number of guests get together and make a quilt or embroider a tablecloth with matching napkins (just about every woman knows how to do the cross stitch). This kind of gift is priceless and will become a family heirloom.

After the gifts have been opened, you might want to make a bonnet out of the bows and ribbons from the presents (use a paper plate as the headpiece and attach the ribbons to tie the hat on). It's lots of fun and makes for memorable silly pictures.

If you want to give out souvenirs, you do not have to go through a party store or wedding planner. Many Greek or Italian family events feature Jordan almonds wrapped in pastel tulle and tied with a commemorative ribbon (John and Sally, February 14, 2026). You can buy the Jordan almonds at the supermarket or a wholesale club, or even online, the tulle by the yard, and just pay to have the ribbon printed. This should keep the mementos cost down.

You can also go to your local dollar store where you should be able to find beautiful, mementos appropriate for a wedding (vases, candleholders, small boxes, many of which have angels or flowers on them) or baby's birth (all manner of ceramic items, such as blue or pink booties, teddy bears, bottles).

Bachelor/Bachelorette Parties

These parties usually take place the night before, or the weekend before the wedding. They are usually the responsibility of the best man or the maid/matron of honor, although a sibling is often corralled into helping at the last minute. The bridal party is expected to share the cost and planning of these parties, but often doesn't.

Therefore, it is also true that bachelor and bachelorette parties can be very expensive and extremely humiliating. Too many bad movies have given many people unreal expectations of what kind of party this should be, and those hosting one are often inexperienced at throwing a party to begin with.

These parties should be well planned, because there is usually a lot of drinking, and they can often last until the wee hours of the morning. Whoever hosts a bachelor party should make sure that the guests have eaten dinner, because drinking on an empty stomach can be dangerous, especially if guests are driving.

A few bachelorette parties I've attended started after dinner (around 8:00 or 9:00 p.m.), but I would suggest an earlier start so that food is involved, and perhaps you'll have an earlier evening overall (especially if the wedding is the next day). Even if you were planning on going out on the town later on, I would suggest an easy to prepare a meal of lasagna, salad and garlic bread (homemade or ordered from a local deli). Or just order in pizza!

Invitations to this kind of party are usually made by Evite or over the phone. Most bachelorette parties consist of the bridal party, a few female family members who must be invited (such as the groom's sister-in-law), and the bride's best friends, so it's usually not more than 20 people and often somewhere between eight and 16.

The most popular way to throw a bachelor party is to do it in a restaurant or bar. Men tend to rent out back rooms, which can be outrageously expensive (I'd rather just give the couple cash), or meet at places like Hooters, or go bar hopping to strip clubs. Women tend to go to a favorite restaurant, club, or perhaps a Chippendales-like establishment. This kind of evening can run each participant hundreds of dollars (because you always treat the groom or bride-to- be) and, if only one or two people are paying, this kind of party can run a tab well over $2000. Many bridal party throwers are shellshocked by the cost of the night before party.

When my husband was tapped for best man service, he called around to see how much dinner at a men's club would be for the guys and quickly decided that the $2000 tab was just too much so I offered him our home (my son and I stayed at my mom's for the night) and the guys grilled steaks, smoked Cuban cigars, played poker, watched a porn video or two, and then disbanded around 2:00 in the morning. I doubt the party cost more than $400 and everyone was happy.

If there's no home to have this kind of party in, renting a hotel room for the night is the next best thing. There's no cleaning up, but you do have to bring a number of things to the hotel room, such as the booze and plates (unless you want to order everything from room service, and that's just about as expensive as going to a restaurant) and cart them all home again. You can avoid ordering food from room service by ordering pizza or Chinese takeout or using UberEats or DoorDash. Do not let the hotel know that you are having a party in your room because they will want to charge you a corking fee for your booze.

Guys don't give gifts at bachelor parties, but they may bring a bottle. Women tend to bring intimate items for the bride, like racy lingerie or funny sex-related items (chocolate body parts, come to mind). Although I didn't have a cake at my bachelorette party (which consisted of a night of visiting my favorite bars in Greenwich Village), I have been to a few bachelorette parties were cake was served (this is the homemade party version) and the cake itself is often a novelty item (those body parts again). One simple recipe for this kind of cake is to make a round vanilla or chocolate cake, stand a Twinkie or devil dog in the center, and then cover with peach or chocolate icing.

Home and hotel parties for the bachelor often feature a visit from a stripper, which is always more expensive than expected. The guys usually chip in for this amongst themselves, but the stripper expects a nice tip, and may charges a travel fee as well.

My husband got hoodwinked into attending a bachelor party that involved a night of going to strip clubs in New York City. The party started in the guy's house, but headed downtown around midnight, but only a few of the guys knew they were going to be doing this, so few of them had a lot of cash on them. This turned out to be a very expensive evening for everyone who attended, especially because someone had to keep tipping the strippers for paying extra attention to the groom-to-be.

My son was recently made the "blade of honor" for a bachelorette party for a woman who he has played Dungeons and Dragons with. He decided that they would play laser tag under the influence. There are many different ways to do this now so be creative (and save money!)

Anniversary Celebrations

The anniversary party should be as extravagant as you can afford, but still not outrageously expensive. I was 24 years old when I threw my parents their 25th wedding anniversary party, and pretty close to dirt poor. Yet, through the network of family and my parents' good friends, we managed to put together a party that was as elegant as they could have imagined.

I knew I could never afford the lavish restaurant anniversary parties that some of my parents' friends' kids were throwing. One couple had their's at Tavern on the Green in Central Park, and asked their friends to kick in a per-couple fee, that included the meal and the gift. But that approach has never been right for me. Miss Manners says that if you do the inviting, you should do the paying. I just decided that making it a surprise party would be the extra ingredient. So I "borrowed" my mother's address book one afternoon and invited all of my parents' friends, both old and new, including my mom's maid of honor and my dad's best man, whom he hadn't seen for years. The party took place at my aunt's house (she offered). The coup de grace was that I flew my younger brother in from California for the weekend.

The menu consisted of all my parents' favorite things to eat and drink. We made some dishes ourselves and had other items catered.

My aunt knew that my mother had recently developed a passion for Lladro figurines, so she collected a small fee from the guests (she was the invite contact), and bought a Lladro sculpture of a bride and groom as the big anniversary present for my parents. Most anniversary parties features some big present from the guests. It can be anything from a lovely piece of crystal to a cruise.

My aunt arranged to have music from the late 50s playing (my parents were married in 1958) and knew just the right songs to play. The guests all danced and reminisced, and it was a wonderful party on a budget.

A nice touch for an anniversary party is to order a sheet cake and have the baker use a photo from the couples' wedding as the decoration on the cake. You can also order a three- tiered cake and use the wedding centerpiece from their original wedding cake or buy them a new one.

Another idea for the joint present is to ask each guest to bring an old photo of themselves with the anniversary couple, and to write something about them. One woman painstakingly put this together on her computer and ended up creating a cherished momento book for the anniversary couple, and the guests who attended the party.

Another unique and inexpensive idea for mementos is to have a wedding photo of the couple reproduced and laminated, so that you have a placemat that can be used at the anniversary party and then take it home when the guests leave. You could also make T-shirts or coffee mugs through Vista or iPrint.

One anniversary party featured a slideshow of the couples' wedding photos, with a commentary by the bridal party. This is a good way to bring back the memories without having to pass the wedding album around.

I attended a 10th anniversary party for a couple who had eloped. This time around they wanted to throw themselves as big a party as they could, so they had an outdoor party under tents in their very large backyard (they were at least 100 people there). The food was catered, and a hired band supplied the entertainment. It was like a wedding reception, but much more laid-back.

Another way to have a large anniversary party is to go back to the hall where a couple first had the reception. If you can, you might even try to reproduce the original menu and music, but this could be very expensive.

Bon Voyage Party

Anniversary parties sometimes turn into a bon voyage party, because the group gift is often a trip—a special trip that the couple has always wanted to go on. I know of one couple who had five kids, and had never managed to go to Greece, where their parents were from. The kids got together and sent them to Greece for their 30th anniversary as their present.

One way of making two tickets to a foreign country affordable is to get family and/or friends to "donate" airline mileage points to one sibling and then have them cash them in for two tickets. This is a lot of work, and will probably take a solid half day on the phone, but two round-trip tickets to Europe usually runs at least $1500, so it's definitely worth it if you don't have cash.

At a bon voyage party, the decorations should be themed. If you plan to buy decorations and unique place settings, try to go online or visit your local party stores for pricing because these are the kinds of items that are often on close-out at one store and full price at another. You might be able to find decorations that are perfect for your party (such as palm trees, beaches, etc.), which are much better than a generic bon voyage.

If you want to make your decorations, it can be something as simple as blue table cloths, to represent water with cardboard fishes glued to them, and a cake in the shape of a boat if the party recipients are going on a cruise or a light blue tablecloth with white clouds and little toy airplanes on the cake.

For the more complicated version of the bon voyage party, you could do something as inspired as an amateur luau for a trip to Hawaii or feature a menu from the country where the recipient is going (go online to search for recipes) and artistic renderings of the country's landscape or monuments. You can find images of architectural wonders and tape them to the wall (such as the Eiffel Tower or the Pyramids). If you are one of those truly inspired party throwers (or if you have already done this a few times for children) you could make a piñata in the shape of the architectural wonder and fill it with candy from that country (the Leaning Tower of Pisa with Perugia chocolates). You could also try to do the same with the cake. Don't forget to play music from the country to be visited (which you should be able find on Spotify).

Sometimes people bring presents to these parties, sometimes they don't. Sometimes a collection is taken to buy the party recipient a new set of luggage. Another appropriate gift is a collection of travel related items, such as travel size toiletries, books to read on the plane, or make up and jewelry travel cases. You might also give a little something from the place being visited, such as candy, to whet the visitors appetite.

Graduation and Retirement Parties

Graduation and retirement parties appear to be opposite ends of the life spectrum, but are actually very similar—graduation parties represent retirement from a certain phase of schooling. They are also attended by people who have been through the trenches together—other graduating students, and others in the workplace.

Because students in the class all graduate on the same day, you have to make sure that your favorite classmate's graduation party isn't scheduled for the same day as your's. By coordinating parties, you might even be able to get a few students together to share the bill. However, many graduation parties include the families who helped foot the graduate's bill through school, so be careful not to mix the wilder "I'm finally done with law school" bash with the more staid family affair.

Graduation usually entails two parties—the bash and the family celebration. The bash is usually thrown by a few students chipping in and features the ubiquitous kegs of beer, jugs of wine, chips and dip, and possibly pizza ordered in. Keep it simple and keep it plastic, because the partying is the focus not the food or the décor.

The family celebration is a much more formal gathering—aunts and uncles you haven't heard from since the bar mitzvah, second and third cousins twice removed—are all descending upon the graduate with presents of Parker pen sets and envelopes of cash or gift cards. Invitations to graduation parties usually come by phone or Evite. Some may even be cleverly designed to resemble a diploma.

If it's an at-home celebration, the party should take place on a Saturday afternoon, so relatives from not too far away can drive in for the day. It will probably be semi-catered, featuring the big sandwich, hot plates of ziti and lasagna and meatballs, salad, bread, and a sheet cake with the word "congratulations!" spelled out in icing. If the party takes place in June (which is when most schools let out), it could be in the backyard, and might be a barbecue. Beer and soda can be set out in coolers.

If there's any decoration, it tends to be white and blue (don't ask me why), although some creative parents or friends may try to coordinate the décor with the school's colors. One graduation party featured fancy paper napkins rolled up as though they were diplomas and tied with ribbons.

For a centerpiece, you could buy one of the mini character graduate figures (such as the Barbie graduate doll or Mickey and Minnie, or even Precious Moments). If the graduate collects these kinds of mementos, you could buy a graduation figure, and give it to them at the end of the celebration.

You can also make a centerpiece that is relevant to the profession the graduate plans to enter—for a doctor or nurse, a basket stuffed with inflated surgical gloves, bandages, a thermometer, etc., that you can put together from almost any medical cabinet or a simple visit to the local pharmacy. Same goes for an architect (rulers, pencils, larger erasers), or lawyer (a copy of the *Law Review*, yellow legal pads, stenographer's, tape). It's easy to put something together to reflect almost any profession.

The one thing I would caution against giving is the pen set since the graduate will get a ton of these. I dislike giving money (because I want to give a personal, memorable gift), but this is an occasion where I often do. It's also a good occasion to give a gift certificate, or even a treasury bond.

When someone retires, they often get two parties—one at work, and another one with family, friends, and co-workers.

The work party can be as formal as a sit-down dinner for 100 to toast the life work of the retiree, who is then given an engraved gold watch or a crystal bowl. Or it can be a dinner at a favorite restaurant near the job after the last day of work, where the co-workers get together and chip in for a last meal together. They usually buy something a little more fun like luggage (for that trip the retiree is planning) or art supplies for that hobby that they will supposedly now have more time for, or even a gift certificate or gift card. Then there's lots of hugging, lots of kissing, some crying, and lots of photos.

When my father retired from consistory after 25 years of service at the local church, the other consistory members threw him a dinner party for 50. A champagne punch was served on the church lawn as a guests arrived. A bulletin was printed with the three-course menu, which also served as a momento of the occasion.

The meal was extravagant in its presentation (melon and prosciutto, sliced London broil with mushrooms, string beans and carrots, individual lemon and berry tarts), because one of the newer consistory members was an amateur chef. After a performance of piano music and a recital of Broadway songs (another consistory member was a professional singer), speeches were made and my father was prevented with a sculpture of the tree of life for his current contributions to the church. It was a warm and touching party, and truly elegant.

However, it is usually the party with family and friends, typically thrown by the spouse or the adult kids, that really marks the entry into retirement. It usually includes a number of work related friends or associates from over the years. It can be in a restaurant or at home and usually takes place in the afternoon or evening, featuring either lunch or dinner. Cocktails or punch are served. Numerous toasts are made.

I know some adult siblings who hosted a retirement party for their mother, who was a nurse. They were able to use the community room at the local hospital where she worked. They made a centerpiece out of hospital supplies and asked each of their mothers' friends to bring something, such as a salad or dessert. It was an extremely successful celebration.

If you are invited to a retirement party, always check to see if there is a collection for a big gift for the retiree before you go out and buy something on your own. Generally, a gift that relates to the retiree's hobby is very appropriate. It could be something as simple as two tickets to a local movie theater (most theater chains sell gift cards), or some books that you know the person will enjoy. It could even be an IOU for a lunch in the near future, when the change in the pace of the retiree's life begins to settle in.

When I was younger, I took many of these "Hallmark" life occasions, and the parties that marked them, for granted. Now that I've been through a handful of these life experiences myself, and find myself either hosting the special occasion celebrations, or at least participating in them, I realize how important they are. These are the times we remember, so make the details count.

Chapter Six: Parties for Friends and Family

Most of us have annual get togethers and family obligations that we are responsible for. In my family, I'm the one who hosts the holiday dinners—Thanksgiving, Christmas, and Easter—because my mother was a minister and always had to work on those days. I have a close friend who has a wonderful trim the tree party every December, and a cousin through marriage who invites us for a spectacular Fourth of July party every year.

Before I took over my family traditions, I remember visiting my father's sister's house in Connecticut for the holidays, but we always celebrated Greek Easter (which usually falls the week after the traditional Easter) with my mother's sister in Riverdale. When I think of each side of my family, it is those annual holiday gatherings that are the basis for most of my childhood family memories.

This also happened with the family I married into—my mother-in-law loved to host New Year's Eve and it "belonged" to her for many years. I hope that my son will cherish the memory of these the family gatherings as well as I have.

Since I know that every year I will be serving Thanksgiving, Christmas, and Easter dinner, I have linen and dishes and decorations galore (bought on sale the day after the holiday) for each holiday. I actually remember debating whether or not I should buy myself a porcelain Easter salt and pepper shaker set that featured pink and blue eggs nestled in a white basket. It was on sale for half price for $8 30 years ago and it was a one day only sale. It seemed awfully pricey for something I was only going to use once a year, but I decided to treat myself and it has become one of my favorite Easter table pieces (and I've certainly recouped the price).

My rule for seasonal entertaining is that if you are the person who hosts the annual get togethers, the cost of special decorations will be displaced over the years. You should feel good about investing in appropriate decorations that may become family heirlooms as the years go by.

The basics for any given holiday are a tablecloth and a centerpiece. Discretion is then advised regarding how many accents you want to add, such as the above-mentioned salt and pepper shakers, decorative platters, cookie jars, and mugs. One way to ensure that your holiday décor will always be plentiful is to let people know that you love adding to the existing table. You will then most likely receive decorative housewares as presents when guests visit for the holidays. However, you can only use a finite number of platters for any holiday

I do try to have one really spectacular element each year that will set each holiday apart from the previous one. One year I made scores of Christmas cookies, which I decorated, shellacked, and gave out as Christmas ornaments. Another year I let the kids string tree garland of popcorn and cranberries. I made my own gingerbread house at Christmas (or at least I tried, which was fun in itself). One Easter, I hid eggs with fancy candy inside for adults. And this year I created an Easter egg hunt of Ferraro chocolate eggs for my grown son!

Christmas

This is a big holiday time of the year for me, and since I have a large extended family, as did my husband, we tend to celebrate the holiday season by having big and a little get togethers throughout the month of December. As a result, I begin to decorate my house the first week of December (whether or not I have the tree up).

I also run a business, and host at least one office holiday party a year, often combo shopping for the two parties at once (and thus saving money by buying in bulk).

I have multiple Christmas themed tablecloths. One is a hand-me-down from my grandmother that always reminds me of holidays at her house, but it's also the less spectacular of all of them. Another is one I put on when young children are coming because I don't care about it as much as the others. I also have a rather expensive green tablecloth with gold and red Christmas tree embroidery on it that I received as a present and have used every year since it was given to me.

Since we have so many holiday gatherings, a Christmas tablecloth adorns the dining room table throughout the season (and is washed frequently). If you entertain a lot during the season, I would recommend that you buy at least two Christmas tablecloths and alternate them. I would also recommend that you case the department and discount stores and price the Christmas tablecloths before the holiday. Pick out the ones you want, and then go shopping the morning after the holiday or online. It is almost certain to be there at half price on the 26th.

The other thing you can do is buy green and red tablecloths (or fabric) and napkins and alternate them (green tablecloth with red napkins). If you're at all artistic, and want to embroider a simple Christmas tree or wreath in the corners and along the border in gold, this can really dress up your tablecloth.

Another alternative is to buy winter-themed tablecloths (snow covered village scenes, snowmen with some snow falling), which you can use for the holidays and throughout the winter months. Yards of dark fabric, in navy blue or the purple, can also be used, perhaps with a lace runner.

I have a full collection of Christmas tableware that I have amassed over the years. Some have been gifts, others I have bought for myself, and some I have found at thrift shops. I use them all. In my family, I am considered one of the Christmas queens.

My Christmas collection consists of a full set of dishes for eight, which were a present, as well as a set of glasses and mugs (also presents), a Santa cookie jar, and an illuminated ceramic Christmas tree. We have a special plate where we placed the cookies for Santa on Christmas Eve (bought on December 26th for $3) when my son was a child, three platters, candlesticks, a teapot, and a ceramic bread basket. The bread basket and candlesticks, or the cookie jar, are usually my centerpieces. I consider this to be a fairly full table and rarely put all this Christmas fare out at the same time.

However, I list these items and suggestions for family presents as well, because you can usually pick them up at after-Christmas sales and save them for the next year. Occasionally you may be able to find a Lenox Christmas piece for sale at a yard sale or flea market. Buy it and give it to someone who loves Christmas. They won't care if it's used, because these items can go for up to $100 new.

I don't like to clutter my house with too many Christmas knickknacks. Aside from my Christmas tree, I put a reusable wreath on my door, a Christmas towel in my guest bathroom, and I hang the Christmas cards I received around the fireplace mantle.

Although my Christmas wreath is store-bought, my mother used to make beautiful Christmas wreaths to sell at the local school fair, and everyone bought them. She would buy Styrofoam bases from an arts and craft or floral supply store, and then glue on acorns, pinecones, "itchy balls," and walnuts and spray paint the whole thing gold. She would finish the wreath with a glued on red velvet bow. You can also make candlestick wreaths this way.

The towel I put in my guest bathroom at Christmastime is also handmade. Someone took a red towel and stitched a cut-out of a green Christmas tree to the terrycloth. It adds a nice touch to the holiday season.

I host a number of get-togethers and parties over the Christmas season from breakfast to dessert, and attend a few gatherings as well.

One of my best friends hosts an annual trim-the-tree dinner around the third week of December. Guests bring ornaments for her tree and we decorate the tree while we eat. She always makes a homemade eggnog and the food is usually a spread of pasta, salad, vegetables, and various hors d'oeuvres. Everything is served on red and green plastic plates.

I usually host a buffet for extended family and their kids before Christmas, during which we exchange gifts. Because the holiday season is so hectic, this party is often on Friday night. Since we all have so many events to attend this time of year, I might ask some of my guests to bring dessert or a side dish. I usually serve some sort of casserole, salad, and garlic bread, and then a big desert spread with a pie and homemade cookies. I might buy the seasonal ice cream cake that is featured at the local Carvel or Baskin Robbins for the kids.

I love cooking the Christmas dinner, but I am also usually exhausted from the shopping and wrapping of the days before. Therefore, I always make the same meal, because I can do it with my eyes closed: turkey, Greek salad, stuffed celery, mashed potatoes, and stuffing with the leftover desserts from the other parties during Christmas week. I might add some store-bought baklava ($12 at the local Greek store or at Costco, which feeds 12). I stock plenty of sparkling apple cider at this time of year.

I have collected an assortment of Christmas music which spans the standards of Handel's *Messiah* to Perry Como/Bing Crosby classics to Christmas rock 'n' roll and rap. I play these old CDs on an old fashioned stereo as background music throughout the gatherings. I have been doing this for years.

Some people don't like to have the same Christmas party year after year. Thankfully, there are many variations on the Christmas theme. I've read of Christmas fiestas, where the food featured is Mexican (do it yourself fajitas and quesadillas) with a holiday piñata for the kids. In the Caribbean, people don't celebrate Christmas on Christmas Day but Christmas Eve, or the arrival of the Three Kings. The meal is traditionally a roasted pig (pernil) with meat pies, rice, and plantains. There are even special candies reserved especially for this time of year, such as Spanish nougat (*Turron*).

Other Christmas party variations include Christmas luaus (lots of pineapple and coconut drinks, and menu items), a Tex-Mex Christmas (barbecued ribs and refried beans), or a Victorian Christmas party (plum putting, lace doilies around a Christmas tea).

You could also serve traditional Christmas foods from around the world. Try everything from a French log cake to English Christmas puddings.

Thanksgiving

For me, Thanksgiving is a lot like Christmas, except I have the whole day to prepare.

I've been making the Thanksgiving dinner since I was 22 years old, but it wasn't until I had a child that I broke down and bought myself a Thanksgiving tablecloth. I am so glad I did. I can't tell you the number of white linen tablecloths that were ruined by gravy and/or wine stains because I was unable to accept that I would probably be doing this holiday for the rest of my life. Being frugal, I didn't want to just buy a tablecloth for the one day, so I waited until I found a perfect fall tablecloth, which is green, mustard, and orange, with leaves and threads of gold. Very classy, as well as being practical and cheap (I think I paid $7 for it decades ago). Also, it's easy to clean and hard to stain. I also bought some pilgrim candles and candlesticks at the local dollar store many years ago, as well as various pumpkins that I use for both Thanksgiving and Halloween.

Fall is a wonderful time of year for fruit and vegetables that make great food as well as interesting art. Martha Stewart's simple carved apple candleholders are perfect for the Thanksgiving centerpiece. Just hollow out most of a polished apple's core (and sprinkle with lemon juice afterwards so the apple doesn't turn brown) and use it as a candlestick.

You can also dress up the table with an artistically laid out array of fall vegetables, such as small gourds and pumpkins, corn on the cob, and apples. A linen-lined basket of homemade bread also makes a nice centerpiece for this holiday.

I have a large white platter with a turkey embossed on it that I always use on Thanksgiving. When my son was younger, I put his Thanksgiving art on display—the turkey handprint, or a feathered turkey.

My Thanksgiving meal is as traditional as it gets, and rarely varies. I make a turkey, cornbread stuffing, cranberry sauce, mashed potatoes, and baked sweet potatoes, Greek salad, stuffed celery, and a pumpkin pie with whipped cream for dessert. The local supermarket where I shop offers a free turkey with a $200 purchase, a deal no cheapskate can turn down. You could also often get turkey for as little as $.39 a pound in 2026 during the holidays.

As with Christmas, it's not hard to vary the traditional for something different for this holiday. You could try to make your meal even more authentic, finding Colonial recipes (I believe the first thanksgiving had a lot more fish than we realize) or interesting recipe variations for the traditional ingredients of turkey, cranberries, pumpkin, and cornmeal. You could even replace the turkey with other fowl, such as goose, duck, Cornish, hens, quail, or even pheasant, or try a vegetarian Thanksgiving, or Turducken (a deboned chicken stuffed inside a deboned duck, which is then stuffed inside a deboned turkey, with layers of stuffing between each bird--this did not work for me). The Internet is a great place to find recipe variations. Epicurious.com featured 16 different Thanksgiving recipes from Colonial Boston to Shaker.

Easter

When I think of Easter, I think of spring flowers, egg hunts, and sumptuous Easter baskets. I believe these elements should be part of this holiday, whether or not it has any religious significance for you, and regardless of whether there are children around.

Since my mother was a minister, I always spent Easter morning in church. The church I attended had a policy whereby you could buy an

Easter lily to decorate the altar on Easter Sunday ($15 each), and then take it home after the service. I thought this was a nice way to make a donation to my church and have a beautiful plant in your home for the rest of spring.

But if your church doesn't do something like that, or you don't go to church, you can always go to Aldi's or Target and get spring plants for your Easter table.

My Easter table is decorated by a pastel tablecloth of pink, lavender, blue, and white squares with matching napkins. I use these linens all spring. I have two ceramic Easter baskets made by a family friend in which I place Easter eggs and fresh bread, and salt and pepper shakers. It's a fairly simple table, but always looks lovely and very springlike.

Spring is a time of pastel colors and the table cover can be any combination of shades of lavender, purple, yellow, peach, etc. Flowers make a beautiful centerpiece this time of year, from the more traditional Easter lilies and lilacs, to simple daisies and even wildflowers. Baskets lined with pastel fabric (or a linen napkin) and brimming with dyed eggs, fresh baked bread, or fruit (especially strawberries) are wonderful table accents.

My Easter dinner is pretty standard and much the same every year, but I believe everyone looks forward to it. I roast a leg of lamb with garlic and oregano and serve it with oven-browned potatoes, the famous Greek salad, Greek cheeses and olives, cheese pies, and grape leaves stuffed with rice (store-bought).

A baked ham, another traditional Easter entree, can sometimes be obtained free with a purchase of $200 or more at a local supermarket, or bought for about $6 this time of year. (so I will often buy two, freeze one and make pea soup from the leftovers!)

Dessert can be fruit pies, or you might want to try something a little ethnic, such as baklava or Italian pastries. Sugar cookies in the shape of bunnies always go over well, even with adults. You can buy cookie cutters at a discount store or make your own designs out of cardboard (but these can't be used year after year).

Many families have a tradition of dying eggs for this holiday. My son and I usually spend an evening during Easter week applying store-bought color dyes, and commercial stickers to at least a dozen eggs that I've hard boiled (buy two dozen at the wholesale store). I really doesn't matter what size these eggs are because they are mostly for display. I buy my dyes and stickers at the dollar store and save what I don't use for the next year. However, you can make the same Easter egg dyes as those sold commercially by adding a few drops of vinegar and food coloring to a glass of water.

One of the centerpieces of my Easter table is a basket filled with the Easter eggs we have dyed. Before the night is over, we put some of the hard-boiled eggs in the salad. We have a Greek tradition of egg smashing that is supposed to bring good luck to the one whose egg holds up the best. So we smash each other's eggs (one at a time, first one side, then the next), and the one with the least damaged egg will have the best luck. We then put the eggs in the salad.

Since I usually have at least two dozen boiled eggs, I serve deviled eggs as an appetizer on this holiday. You can dress up deviled eggs by adding caviar or smoked bacon bits on top of the filling. We also have a lot of egg salad for lunch the days following the holiday, and I often give out eggs to guests as they are leaving.

When my son was young, we would have an Easter egg hunt in the morning when he woke up. I would buy at least a dozen plastic Easter eggs and put almost anything inside: chocolate covered eggs, gold coins, miniature peanut butter cups, or jellybeans. Easter egg hunts for adults can feature pieces of paper with prizes, fortunes placed in the eggs, or expensive chocolates, such as Perugina.

There is no reason to resort to a store-bought Easter basket, unless you don't have the time to put one together. You could pick up a basket at the dollar store, and Easter grass is usually about a dollar a bag. When my son was young I would fill his basket with small items from the dollar store: superman comics, a Spalding ball, a paddle and balls, silly putty, bubbles. You might want to make your own cookies and put a few in. I would wrap the whole basket with tinted cellophane and tie it with a ribbon. I would reuse the basket every year.

My mother tells of how my artistically inclined grandmother used to make Easter baskets out of cookie dough and fill them with dyed eggs, Easter chocolate, an orange, and one special toy, such as a small doll.

One of my neighbors would give my son an Easter basket every year, so I have kept these baskets and use them throughout the house. We use one for ripening fruit in our kitchen; another for notepads, pens, tape, and scissors near the kitchen phone (yes, I still have a land line); and one in each bathroom to hold brushes, combs, and other grooming supplies. I also save them to put together my own gift baskets, sometimes for Valentine's Day and birthdays.

Adult Birthday Parties

Adult birthday parties are usually thrown to mark a special birthday, such as a 40th or 65th. I don't remember going to a lot of birthday parties before my friends and I started hitting 30. I think this was because we were self-conscious about throwing our own parties, and had not yet found someone we could get to do it for us, and we were all pretty broke living in New York City.

Thirtieth and 40th birthday parties are especially fun. They should be a little wacky and truly memorable. One of the ways to do this is to try to make the party a surprise, although the recipient often has an inkling that it's coming. If you do manage to make it a true surprise, you get extra points.

I was the first in my crowd to turn 30, so my husband threw me a "surprise" party (although I was suspicious because he got two of my good friends to take me out to dinner on a Saturday night to keep me occupied while he put it all together). My husband managed to round up a number of friends I had not seen since college, which was a real joy, and one of my high school friends brought old pictures, which we were thrilled to look at.

The menu was pretty easy, because people would be coming and going over a long period of time. My husband made his famous four-alarm chili, salad, and bread, and margaritas for one and all (my favorite drink). He ordered an ice cream cake, which I like, because it feeds so many.

Two years later, it was his turn, and I really wanted to make his 30th party a surprise, so I had it in my office (I own my own business), which was in an apartment, so I had a kitchen. I made tons of chicharrones de pollo (Dominican fried chicken), which is delicious hot or cold, rice and beans, and salad. I filled the bathtub with beer on ice and brought huge jugs of white and red wine, and had a sheet cake. I got in touch with friends my husband haven't seen in years and invited most of the people he worked with. The party would've been a complete surprise if the doorman hadn't asked my husband if he was going to the party on his way in.

One of the things that turned out to be quite funny was the opening of the presents. I had invited a number of my husband's cousins and they brought him gag gifts like Polident, Depends, and Grecian Formula 409. I always do this now when I'm invited to a 30th birthday party (by the 40th it's not so funny).

I also threw my husband a surprise birthday party when he turned 35, because I knew he wasn't expecting it. I threw it on the weekday his birthday fell on, and invited only a few close friends, but I flew his mother in from Miami. It was quite a surprise.

My mother threw my father a surprise party when he turned 40. I remember her hiding bottles of booze behind the curtains and conspiring with friends to get him out of the house while she prepared everything. He kept on asking her why she had so much food that he liked, and she kept on making up inane answers, but he believed them, and was surprised.

Getting the birthday boy or girl out of the house is often one of the most difficult parts of throwing a surprise party. So something like tickets to a ball game (as a birthday present) is a nice way to circumvent this, as are conspiracies with friends and relatives (shopping spree, mother/daughter lunch).

For my best friend's husband's 40th birthday, she planned a surprise "this is your life" party," complete with written memories from friends that were bound into a book. She had coordinated this by mail months in advance.

Other friends have marked the coming of their 40th birthday with an all-day adults-only excursion, such as a weekend in Atlantic City or Las Vegas, a day at a spa, a golf marathon, hiking, or even deep-sea fishing. Less expensive ways to do something like this are to find group rates for things like a day at the local amusement park or a Broadway play or even the big summer movie. It's fun to experience these kind of things in an adult group (the last time you did something like this was probably high school), and you won't easily forget what you did on that birthday.

You can also have a kids-themed party for an adult at home, with party hats, goody bags, and childish games like pin the tail on the donkey and musical chairs for adults. Maybe even spin the bottle (it depends on your crowd). Don't forget to make ice cream sodas!

For my husband's 35th birthday party, we had a Batman theme. We had Batman plates and napkins, a Batman piñata, and I believe we even had a Batman ice cream cake and Batman party hats.

I had a colleague who was an avid Star Trek fan, and went on the Star Trek cruise every year. One year he shared with me that he had bought the Star Trek Monopoly game, but had never played it. So I conspired with some of our friends to throw him a Star Trek birthday party, with food loosely based off of various Star Trek episodes. I asked participants to buy him Star Trek related gifts, and we all played Star Trek Monopoly to great enjoyment.

By the time my dad reached 60, we wanted to throw him an elegant birthday party. He loved to dance, so we found a Hilton Hotel nearby that had a live band on Friday and Saturday nights and booked a table for 30. We invited his very best friends (many of whom had already retired and moved to Florida) and had a black-tie party that was quite fancy, like a small wedding. My uncle (retired to Florida) sent him a singing birthday telegram, which he adored (we had to clear it with the Hilton first because they were afraid she would be a stripper). My mom, brother, and I split the cost which was about $60 a couple more than 30 years ago.

For my mom's 65th birthday, we had a party for 100 in the community room of one of her churches. It was an afternoon buffet with a sheet cake and champagne punch. Presents for this party were often senior citizen-related, but fun, such as a book about deals you can you can't get if you're over 50, or the New York City discount fare card (I did the paperwork for her), an AARP membership, and lots of discount tickets she could only get once she was 65.

I did not have a 65th birthday party, but a 64th. I had a Beatles-themed "When I'm 64" party, complete with a Beatles tribute band. All the food was somehow Beatle-themed, such as apple martinis and a strawberry fields dessert. I asked everyone to come in '60's clothing and we danced until 11 o'clock. I rented the community room of my co-op and had 35 guests. It cost me about $1500, but it was so well worth it!

Family Reunions

While whole books have been written about planning family reunions, I think it's possible to sum up the strategy for making these big family gathering successful—plan every detail, and make sure you have enough activities to do. Then have a backup plan in case it rains.

Family reunions are typically attended by between 50 and 100 people. While they are occasionally held at the ancestral home (if there's enough land), they are more likely to be held in a national park in the summer (often over the Fourth of July weekend, when everyone will have a long weekend), where family members can camp out, and all the descendants can run free and keep busy. National parks are cheap (a small entry fee for the week, and separate, usually moderate, camping fees) and they come fully stocked with picnic tables, bathrooms, and barbecue grills (not to mention lakes, for swimming, fishing, and canoeing).

Sometimes, a family resort is chosen as a central location (a dude ranch, a hotel in the mountains), where the staff will help you put the reunion together and you can get a group rate. If you go off-season (September or early June) rates are lower. A family reunion should be planned at least six months ahead of time. A lot of the follow-up can be done through email.

One woman asked each branch of the family to send photos and write a brief history, which she put together as a momento. Another family reunion featured a lecture and slideshow on the family history from collected stories and photos. Another family put all the history together, and made their own family version of Trivial Pursuit. Some families have asked everyone for their best or favorite recipes, and put together a family cookbook. One family asked each branch to sew a square for a giant family quilt to be stitched together at the reunion.

Another reunion featured different color T-shirts for each branch of the family (there were five grandparents, each represented by a different color with the first name of the grandparent on the back, so that everyone wearing a purple T-shirt featuring the letter C belonged to Clara's clan).

Food for these large crowds can be an enormous amount of work. If you hold the reunion in a park, you can either make each family responsible for their own food or have different families cook different meals at different times. Everything can be barbecued or cooked on the grill.

Family reunions are a great place to play all those outdoor games you see in old movies—potato sack races, egg rolls, horseshoe pitching, tug-of-war, even croquet, and maybe even pickle ball. Then there's also volleyball, softball, Badminton, and frisbee. You can do group yoga, perhaps even at sunrise or sunset. Of course, the entire reunion should be documented in photos and video. You could also put together scrapbooks for those who attended or make copies of the video.

It's a lot of work to bring many people from different states together every year, and sometimes it's not appreciated if the family members do this too often. One family reunion I know about is held every five years, so that members will make an effort to attend and they can really see the changes in the family over each five year span.

Holidays, birthdays, and family gatherings are the most common reasons why we all get together, but these events should never be taken for granted. Imagination and good planning, can make up for a small budget, and you can create parties that people remember fondly for years.

Chapter Seven: Odd-Occasion Parties

These are the parties that your friends and family will remember until their dying days, and the stories they tell about these events may even become part of the family lore (hopefully it won't be about someone's behavior at one of these parties, but that's another book). These are also the parties that take the most work, because there is so much creativity involved. They should also be the parties that you enjoy the most.

Sometimes these are parties with a purpose, such as raising money for the rent, or moving, and sometimes they're just for the fun of it, like a treasure hunt, or masquerade ball, or a luau. If you love a certain time of year (Halloween or the Fourth of July) or type of dress ('20's, Victorian), these parties can be opportunities to let that fantasy come alive. Some people even tie these parties into a special birthday theme (your husband's birthday set in the StarWar's canteen).

Sweet 16

I'm not sure teenage girls even celebrate this birthday in a big way anymore, but when I remember back to my sweet 16 party, it was my parents who wanted it, not me. It was more a milestone that they were celebrating than one that I was celebrating for myself.

My parents invited 12 of my best friends to our home for a buffet dinner of turkey and a homemade cake with peppermint frosting. Then we all went to see the Broadway play *Grease.* My dad bought me a wrist corsage with 16 pieces of bazooka bubblegum on it. You can easily make this or a variation of it with your daughter's favorite candy wired to fresh or silk flowers on a wrist band.

By the time your daughter hits her teens, the last thing she will want to do is spend her birthday with the family. But Sweet 16 can be a memorable marker, and for many (including myself), it make turn out to be the only large birthday party for her friends during the high school years. The pictures alone will be worth it years from now.

A variation of this theme is the slumber party, usually for a small group (4four to six). One of my best friends from high school had about six of us for a sleepover for her Sweet 16, which was quite memorable, because by 16 we had stopped having slumber parties. Her parents took us to an art gallery opening (very grown-up for us), and then we went back to their house for more grown-up partying and dinner. I remember being very impressed that they had put out an entire spread of appetizers just for us (it was the first time I had Genoa salami and cream cheese roll ups, which I love). Her dad took a terrific, black-and-white group photo of us with our long hair and jeans, mounted it on cardboard, and gave it to us a few weeks later. It was a wonderful momento and I still have it on my dresser after all these years.

Sweet 16 parties can be a wonderful occasion to mark the transition from teen to adult. Now that I'm older, I truly value this marker, and would recommend that parents try to make a special occasion for their daughters, even if it's only a family party with her favorite meal. There is no reason why you can't do this for a son or a non-binary teen as well.

Throwing an adult party for your teenager is one way to make them feel that they are indeed growing up. You could serve a very fancy dinner for their friends (something French or Italian) with the (non-alcoholic) drinks in wine goblets or champagne glasses. Put out the fine linen, china, and silver, and offer a truly elegant dessert of chocolate mousse or a soufflé.

Let your child put together the menu and have the teens all cook it themselves (with your supervision, of course). It can be something as simple as fajitas or as complicated as chicken tarragon. You could also try cooking a new type of cuisine, such as Chinese, Thai, or Japanese, which could be fun. The photos from this party would be prize possessions, so make multiple copies for the friends too.

Other Sweet 16 party ideas could include a makeover party, where friends go to a department store or Sephora and have their make-up done by a professional. Perhaps you also buy each teen a small cosmetic (sometimes department stores have specials where if you buy one item, you get an entire make-up bag of goodies). You could also hire a beauty school student to come to the house for a consultation. Facials, manicures, and pedicures are fun group activities.

Craft Parties

While most of us have been to arts and craft parties for kids, which are always fun because we get to watch children making Christmas ornaments, T-shirts, and ceramics, a well- planned adult craft party is always memorable for both the guests and the hostess.

A traditional type of craft gathering is a quilting party. The hostess must decide on what type of quilt will be made and the pattern. There are so many varieties on quilt making today that the hostess must make this decision before the party. If you need help on deciding, or putting the materials together, there are ample resources online, as well as many quilting books. An easy idea for a quilt party is denim quilts, using pieces of different, worn-out jeans and flannel sheets as the backing.

Most quilting parties require that each guest brings a certain amount of fabric, and then they cut and stitch and trade until the quilts are complete. This takes an afternoon or slightly longer, and a full lunch should be served, which might include salad and sandwiches. If the party has been called to make a quilt for a purpose (such as a bridal or baby shower gift made by friends or family), you might serve a cake with an appropriate motif.

Once known as quilting bees, these parties are the kinds of events that women's groups in the local church used to do on an afternoon before the church fair, and many churches still have craft making afternoons. However, you can do the same thing before a bridal or baby shower and present the bride or mother-to-be with a trove of handmade gifts that are priceless. These include embroidered tablecloths and matching napkins, crocheted or knitted baby clothes, and homemade housewares such as pot holders and tissue box covers. You can get inspiration from craft websites.

Another craft party could involve making Christmas decorations, either to be sold at a local fundraising event or for each participant to take home. The hostess must provide all the basic art supplies and ask each guest to bring something special for the craft, such as feathers, sequins, odd buttons, beads, or glitter to add variety to the decorations. You can make ornaments, wreaths, and even complicated ceramics like a Christmas village, or nativity, which can be ordered from a craft store, and then decorated at the party. You can even make and shellac cookie ornaments. Some women's groups make Christmas pies and fruit cakes and sell or raffle them off at a of bazaar.

When I was a teenager, my aunt belonged to a sewing circle. They would get together monthly to swap patterns and trade material or buy it as a group. They did most of the sewing at home on machines, but they finished the clothing at the circle, taking up hems and sewing in zippers and buttons. They also used the sewing circle to trade buttons and zippers and other stuff, as well as enjoying it as a social gathering.

The kind of party I used to love was getting together with four or five of my girlfriends to tie dye pieces of clothing—anything from T-shirts to bathing suits. For baby boomers, this would make a great activity now, with our own adult kids and grandkids and their friends, or with our now adult friends from our own teenage years.

Tie-dye kits are sold at just about every craft store and you can pick up men's plain white T-shirts for a buck or two at outlets and discount stores. Go through all the white and light colored cotton clothes and stained table linen and sheets you have that you've been meaning to throw out and tie-dye them all. You'd be surprised how interesting things can get. Kids especially just love tie-dyed sheets.

Treasure Hunt

I went to a treasure hunt hosted by a friend of my roommate when I was in college. Clues were placed all over Roosevelt Island (an island in the East River) on the Friday night of a Halloween weekend. Even though it was cold out, and I was running around a part of New York City I was unfamiliar with, in a costume that had high heels and uncomfortable clothing, I had a great time. The host placed clues in the empty community pool, on the inside of a bell, and on the sign of an abandoned insane asylum. It was the kind of setting great slasher movies are based on, and perfect for a Halloween party. The first team to find all the clues got tickets to a Broadway show (it might have been *Rocky Horror*)—I did not win).

There's a really bad '80's teen movie about a treasure hunt called *Midnight Madness*, which inspired my husband and me to throw a Manhattan treasure hunt for our friends when we were in our mid-20s. We invited about 30 people, broke them up into teams of four or five, and had each person put $10 into a kitty that would be the prize for the winning team. We gave them the rules of the hunt at a light cocktail party (lots of appetizers) and gave each team eight dimes for phone calls (it was the '80's). We sent them out into the world at about 3:00 and told everyone to come back to our place by 8:00, whether or not a team had won (where we could give them all dinner—our famous chili).

It took us about two weeks to come up with the clues for the party, which we placed on stickers we attached to objects in public areas. We had to come up with eight New York City locations everyone would know, and then figure out a way to place the clues so that our friends could find them. At a few places, we called the management to ask for help, and if they refused, we just put the stickers (white Avery labels) in the men's and ladies rooms.

The party was a lot of work, but the most fun we ever had. It took us about two weeks to come up with the clues and we spent the entire day before the party running around Manhattan placing clues on landmarks.

We came up with eight locations: Grant's Tomb, P.J. Clarke's, the Port Authority, and Fraunces Tavern were four of them and clues (anagrams, puzzles, word games; one was Scrabble letters in an envelope). The clue for P.J. Clarke's (a famous, old New-York bar) was "Superman in his pajamas, ass backwards." Each team was to call in when they got to the site to confirm. If they couldn't get the clue in an hour, we would give them the next clue, and they would lose a point. The clue to the next site was located somewhere on the site they were calling from. We handed them their first clue (the Scrabble letters in an envelope).

We didn't know how long it would take for a team to figure everything out, but the first team came back around 7:00 p.m. We all had a blast.

You can also put together a scavenger hunt where you give your guests a list of oddball items (a simple list, like a horse, train, cloud, or a weird thing from literature or popular culture like eye of Newt, witch's brew, bell, book, and candle) and give your guests a time limit to bring everything (or a photo on their phone of the items) with rules that all items must be found, not bought. If your hunt is over a holiday, you can make the items coordinate with the holiday theme, such as some sort of Colonial items to tie in with the Fourth of July.

A little creativity in putting the list together will go a long way to making the hunt fun. A great prize as the reward makes people work that much harder and take the whole thing a little more seriously. Cash (the kitty idea), theater tickets, or a gift certificate to a great local restaurant, are all good suggestions for this sort of thing.

Lori Perkins

Masquerades and Costume Parties

I love masquerades and costume parties, but find that as I get older my friends don't throw them anymore. In fact, it is easy to throw a costume party, and relatively inexpensive. The guests, and their costumes, are the theme and the entertainment, although you still have to supply the food and music.

If you're planning on having 25 people or under, throw it in your home. For more than that, rent a small space, like the community room in a co-op. Our co-op hosted a costume party this year, serving mulled wine and cider and roast beef and turkey as the dinner. They had a best costume contest and showed *Rocky Horror* on the big screen TV, which was a great idea. When I was a kid, we used to dunk for apples with dimes in them (it would have to be at least Susan B. Anthony dollars today), which I think would be a riot for adults to do.

You could also have a themed costume party, either tied to the holiday you're celebrating (an Addams Family Halloween party, a Colonial Fourth of July, futuristic New Year's Eve party), or the theme of the party (by decade, a Titanic party, or a Star Trek party, where everyone comes in a Starfleet universe uniform).

I paid to go to a Bridgerton ball in New York City, where I actually rented costumes. It was so much fun to be presented to the Queen's Court, and dance the night away. Of course, you could do something like this on your own for much less (invite me!).

Masquerades are fancy costume parties were everyone is expected to wear a mask and elegant attire or a costume. These are the kinds of parties where you really should send out fancy invitations and hire musicians (or at least a neighborhood kid who can play the violin or piano), and maybe even hire a few teenagers in black pants and white shirts to serve hors d'oeuvres. A spring or summer masquerade could be on the lawn or backyard of a large home (borrowed or rented). While not the least expensive way to entertain, you can keep the cost of an elegant masquerade down by serving punches and the upscale version of the less expensive appetizers (deviled eggs with bacon bits). It is the illusion of elegance that is required here and not the actual receipts on your credit card.

Themed Parties for Adults

The great thing about theme parties is that if you place most of your energy on the theme and its execution, you won't have to spend a lot of money on impressing or entertaining your guests. A successful theme party will do that for you, so you can have a good time.

There are so many varieties for adult parties from the simple (a silly hat party,) to the sublime (a Vegas night). Often a theme party is tied to a birthday, which can be a lot of fun. Just make sure your friends know that there is a theme to the party (I would recommend emailed invitations with conformation for this kind of party), or someone is likely to feel left out. Just in case, you can always keep extra items on hand to include anyone who forgot the theme, such as extra silly hats.

Some simple and successful themes are a pajama party (with breakfast related food, even though the party is at night), a toga party (I understand that the guests are not supposed to wear underwear at the more traditional toga parties, which is why these were so popular on college campuses), a Mardi Gras party (jambalaya, red beans, and rice, pictures of hurricanes) or a fiesta (tacos, nachos, do-it-yourself fajitas, pitchers of margaritas, and a piñata filled with candy or adult prizes).

Decade parties are easy-to-throw theme parties. Guests come in the clothing of the decade, you play the music from the decade, and try to serve the food and drinks from that time. If you have a large screen TV, you can show classic movies from the decade (with the sound turned down, so as not to distract your guests).

A '20's speakeasy party could include guests dressed up as gangsters, gun molls, and flappers with Prohibition-style mixed drinks and bottles of gin on ice in the bathtub. A '30's party could feature dance music and request that guests dress like Fred and Ginger. A '40's party should feature swing music and guests in uniforms from World War II. A '50's party could be a *Happy Days* set, with leather jackets and poodle skirts, burgers and malteds and early rock 'n' roll. For the '60's, a menu of spiked Tang and Cheetos could accompany a soundtrack from the Beatles to the Cowsills (remember them?) with guests in bellbottoms and tie-dyes. The '70's would be a disco party (your own private Studio 54) with pitchers of Harvey Wallbangers, fondue, quiche, and onion dip, leisure suits, and Lycra dresses. You get the idea, I'm sure. Of course, you can go even farther back in time or even to another country (Edwardian England, Revolutionary France).

One woman had a *Casablanca* surprise birthday party for her husband. She had all the guests come in period clothing, rented roulette and poker tables, made armbands for the dealers, borrowed fezzes from a local men's club, had someone playing the piano, and transformed her home into the nightclub from her husband's favorite movie.

Another woman turned her home into a Las Vegas nightclub, with poker and blackjack tables, and music by Elvis, Sinatra, and Cher.

It is easy to come up with a theme around someone's favorite movie, or TV show, from *Star Wars* (reproduce the famous bar scene and buy plates and tablecloths that are made for children's parties) to *Star Trek* (there's even a *Star Trek* cookbook; make your guests improvise those costumes—this could be a riot) to a *Seinfeld* party (you could probably get ideas for this online, but it should be in a crowded apartment with lots of cereal boxes). You could even do a *Lord of the Rings* party for adults.

Other parties I've heard about have been a vintage prom night, where the couples are expected to come in thrift shop prom gowns and tuxedos, wearing corsages. Lots of slow dancing songs are played. Give out tacky prom mementos at the end of the evening. One couple hosted a Valentine's Day party that was black-tie, and had a theme of wine and roses.

Sales Parties

These are really fundraising parties, where you sell your friends things that you hope they will need, or at least want, such as Avon, Mary Kay, Amway, Tupperware, sex toys, or lingerie. I've actually had a good time at some of these parties when I've known ahead of time that I was going to be pitched to. However, when I was invited to one of these without a warning that it was a sales party, it really ticked me off. My rule of thumb: always let your guests know what to expect, preferably with a written invitation. They are more likely to bring money, and credit cards if you let them know ahead of time, which should improve your sales record.

A good sales party we'll have a nice spread for the guests, either appetizers or a late lunch. Because you're asking your guests to spend money, you should make sure that everything looks top quality (so no generic brands on display here).

You should try to have about ten or 12 people at the sales party, including some relatives, who have primed to buy something from you, so that you and your guests won't be embarrassed if nobody buys anything.

I once gave a lecture on writing romantic erotica in the wake of *Fifty Shades of Grey* at a party in Washington DC where the after party was a demo of sex toys by a truly professional salesperson. Champagne was served, the guests had already been loosened up, and the salesperson said it was the most successful party she had ever been invited to. And everyone had fun!

Housewarming Parties

Housewarming party parties can be a lot of fun for both the hosts and the guests. A housewarming party should be by invitation. A lot of people may want to come and see the new house or apartment or co-op (if they've been hearing the details about how you got your mortgage or your move or your renovation), but won't drop by without an invitation. However, many people refrain from throwing housewarming parties because they're afraid it will seem as though they're asking for gifts. If you really don't want gifts, just make an Amazon wish list. People will find it.

You could also have a themed housewarming party, such as home-improvement (where you get tools, gift certificates to the likes of Home Depot and Lowe's) or garden (planters, gardening, tools, plants, seeds).

One couple wanted to have a casual after dinner housewarming party where friends could drop by anytime from 7:00 to 11:00 p.m. On the invitation they wrote, "Please 'warm' our new home and enjoy coffee and dessert with us." This way, the guests knew what to expect.

The food for a housewarming can be as simple as the coffee and dessert mentioned above or a big barbecue or potluck supper (this is actually a very good excuse for a potluck). It's really up to you.

Potluck Parties

Potluck dinners and parties have the reputation of being thrown together, almost at the last minute. But the best bring-your-own-food gatherings I've ever attended have always been well-coordinated.

Whether for 12 or 200 (church functions and school socials), a good hostess, or coordinator finds out what people are bringing and makes sure that there are not too many desserts, and no main dishes. If the party appears to be heavy on side dishes, she might ask you to make your famous Greek meatballs, ensuring that there's the right balance of food for the party. The hostess is also responsible for supplying drinks (which includes alcoholic and non-alcoholic beverages, as well as after dinner coffee, and tea) and the table set up.

A potluck gathering for more than a dozen people should be by invitation, and then followed up by phone. The emailed invitation should state that you need to know what the guest is bringing when they RSVP.

As with all dinner parties, great entertaining is in the details. Because your guests are supplying most of the food, you can really splurge on one or two things, such as champagne with dessert or shrimp cocktail appetizers. You can also use the opportunity to prepare a really complicated dessert or appetizer because you don't have to cook the entire meal.

Potlucks are also wonderful for when you really do want to get together with friends, but your schedule is too hectic to take a day to do the cooking. It's nice to share your friends' food at your table and it gives you the opportunity to try different things.

If you're harried for the holidays, and you have a lot of family to invite, a potluck meal could be a new tradition. If you supply the main course (the turkey, ham, or lamb), your guests can round out the meal with fabulous side dishes.

The church I grew up in has an annual potluck supper with the theme "international night." This is a great way to bring people together and to sample a wide variety of delicious food. This concept would also work well for an office potluck during lunch or just after work, especially around the holidays.

Potluck gatherings are a relaxed way to bring friends together, not to mention the least expensive way to entertain.

Chapter Eight: Outdoor Parties

For most of us, outdoor parties are summer gatherings, because that's the only time of the year we can depend on nice weather. While there are those who are quite capable of throwing elegant parties outdoors, such as weddings under tents and fancy catered garden parties, these are not the most economical ways to entertain (although it does save the cost of renting a hall). Most of us use the excuse to be outdoors as an opportunity to make the entertaining more casual, so most outdoor parties I go to, and certainly the ones I host, are barbecues, picnics, or pool parties.

Barbecues

A barbecue can be as simple as a weenie roast on a beach bonfire or a more complicated marinated steak on skewers affair with hired help doing the cooking. It's really up to your needs.

One woman on a frugality group I belong to said she invited family and friends to open fire weenie roasts (bring your own hotdogs and lawn chairs to sit around the fire). The host supplied the sticks, toppings (relish, sauerkraut, ketchup, cheese sauce), and drinks, and marshmallows for dessert.

The same couple regularly hosts potato roasts (foil provided). The foil-wrapped potatoes are placed on open coals that are covered and uncovered by a shovel. Toppings for the potatoes, such as sour cream, cheddar cheese, bacon bits, and jalapeño peppers, are also provided by the host. These roasts are most popular in the fall, with guests sitting around the open fire, sometimes telling ghost stories.

We have barbecues almost every weekend in the summer, starting with Memorial Day, because we have a pool in the city. At the beginning of the summer I'm thrilled to be grilling hamburgers and hotdogs again and making vats of potato salad, but by the Fourth of July, I'm craving variety, and we begin experimenting with easy marinades on chicken and steak and grilling tuna steaks.

I do have basic barbecue meat in the freezer at all times in the summer: ready-made hamburger patties, lots of hotdogs, and buns for both. You can buy packages of 18 hamburger patties at your local wholesale club. I find two-for-one specials on hotdogs at the supermarket all summer long. Hamburger and hotdog buns can be bought at a wholesale club in bulk, and these are often put on BOGO sales as well. American cheese doesn't freeze well so I tend to buy that fresh.

In the summer, I buy big jars of mayonnaise (for all the potato salad and coleslaw) and big bottles of mustard. I also buy lemons by the bag full and boxes of 100 teabags. And keep pitchers of homemade iced tea and lemonade ready at all times. Limeade is great too and it's even cheaper to make than lemonade. Every weekend I also make two to three pounds of potato salad and coleslaw, which is easy to make from scratch and is incredibly delicious. Large cans of baked beans are available at the wholesale club if this is something you like. When corn on the cob is on sale (two or three for $1), I'll buy some and boil it (put a teaspoon of sugar in the water just before you add the corn and only boil for five minutes).

For a slightly more impressive barbecue, I might marinate and grill some steaks, especially if a good cut of meat is on sale. Every year, at the beginning of the summer, Aldi sells a grill box for about $60. It usually includes eight hamburger patties, two sirloin steaks, two chicken breasts, two pork chops, as well as two bacon-wrapped filet mignons. It is the bargain of the summer, and my security blanket for summer meat should someone drop by who I have to impress at a moment's notice.

For dessert, I always make some kind of pie of whatever fruit is on sale—peaches, strawberries, blueberries, even a delicious mixed blueberry and raspberry pie. However, watermelon is a simple and inexpensive treat that everyone loves, as is a fruit salad. Ice cream sundaes are fun and easy too. They can be surprisingly cheap if you buy the ingredients in bulk—walnuts, chocolate syrup, 5 lbs. tubs of ice cream, whipped cream, and maraschino cherries. Serve each ingredient in its own dish—not in the container it came in—and reuse leftover ingredients at the next time.

That's my basic barbecue menu for up to 30 people. For smaller groups, I might marinate chicken or steak in vinegar and tarragon or teriyaki sauce. Almost any oil and vinegar-based salad dressing makes a good marinade. Grilled pork chops or sausages (dipped in honey mustard) are wonderful. If tuna steak is on sale, grill it, and serve over pasta with olive oil and sautéed garlic. One pound can serve six people this way.

Barbecue season is also the time of year when I make sangria and pitchers of margaritas for guests. Therefore, I usually have a few bottles of red wine or jugs of sangria on hand (Carlo Rossi is a great tasting brand, and usually on sale in the 4 L size in the summer), as well as at least one bottle of Jose Cuervo margarita mix (that is actually cheaper making it from than fresh limes and triple sec). I use a cheaper brand of tequila because this is a mixed drink.

I was invited to a 30th birthday party barbecue where the host hired a caterer to grill up the food for them (hamburgers, hotdogs, and chicken), because they wanted to make sure they saw guess who had traveled up to 100 miles for the occasion. While this was a great idea, the caterer was really expensive—and late. I would suggest hiring a local teenager to flip the burgers and preparing some of the food yourself ahead of time. I would ask various good friends and relatives to make a batch of potato salad or coleslaw (give them the recipe if they don't have their own) and just serve ice cream or put out a spread of do-it-yourself sundaes in plastic bowls for dessert.

A good friend and relative was selling her house, so she decided to have a big Fourth of July barbecue in her backyard. She was afraid no one would come, so she invited everyone she knew (and she worked in a busy store). By the end of the day, she must've had 200 people come and go. She asked everyone to bring something, and she got everything from six packs of beer to trays of ice and beans. She hired someone to roast a pig on a spit. (Most Latin butchers who sell whole pigs can recommend where to have a spit made. If you're lucky, someone you know grew up in a Latin home, and may know how to do this). She also had burgers and hotdogs grilling on two separate grills. There was a piñata with candy for the kids and a very large store-bought sheet cake. Everyone had a great time, and the barbecue really didn't cost her that much.

If you are having a large group (40 or more), you might want to borrow a second grill. If you prefer not to be occupied grilling, hire some neighborhood teenagers to do the cooking so that you'll be free to mingle.

Barbecues are also great for family gatherings with lots of kids. If you can get summer games for them (horseshoes, hula hoops, jump rope, even hopscotch or twister), they should have a good time, and you won't have to worry about them messing up or breaking things in the house.

While there are many themes you could have at a barbecue, the one that comes most easily is a luau. You can serve ribs or pork (or a roasted pig), plenty of fruit drinks (with or without the tiny umbrellas), play Hawaiian music in the background, and serve a fruit salad for dessert. You could get your guests to engage in a hula contest, and use a broomstick for a limbo contest.

You could do the same thing along a fiesta or tropical theme or try putting together a barbecue with a Wild West theme (this would actually be great for kids party).

Picnics

People think of picnics, as being very déclassé, but an elegant picnic is an affair to remember, and one that is fairly easy to organize, because you don't have to clean the house.

When I was younger, my standard picnic fare was fried chicken. It wasn't until I was invited to meet some friends for a picnic in Central Park to hear the *1812 Overture* by the New York Philharmonic that I learned that a picnic could be so much more. They brought wine and brie and French bread, sandwiches of salami and more brie, and exotic chicken salads. And grapes. It was delicious, and not much more expensive than the fried chicken I had brought (maybe even cheaper and certainly easier to make).

Now I host an annual picnic under the stars in Van Cortlandt Park, where the Philharmonic plays a free concert every year in July, and I pack a picnic basket of wine and brie, grapes, and chicken salad that we all look forward to. Don't forget the blanket when packing for your picnic.

For a more elegant picnic, use matching tablecloths (they can be vinyl) and bring out the crystal. There are wonderful plastic matching plate sets, which run about $20 for an entire set of four, that you can buy. A spread of chicken salad with tarragon, curried tuna salad, and smoked turkey and brie served on baguettes or pumpernickel bread, summer fruit, and white wine spritzers will dress up the picnic. Bring a thermos of coffee and serve iced coffee with a luscious cake—something like cheesecake with strawberries, or even a store-bought black forest cake.

Pool Parties

I think of these as outdoor cocktail parties—plenty of snacks and drinks, possibly fruity concoctions like virgin piña coladas.

The food at a pool party should be really light, because people will be going in and out of the water, and you don't want anyone to get sick. I'd recommend lots of pretzels and potato chips, and veggie strips, such as carrots, celery, and red and yellow peppers, with a simple, sour cream dip made from a soup mix.

If you're serving lunch, make it light too—perhaps a large Caesar salad with grilled chicken, or a Cobb salad, or simple sandwiches of tuna or chicken salad, or a homemade gazpacho. I wouldn't have a barbecue until the evening when people won't be swimming as much.

In the summer, ice cream makes a fantastic dessert. You can get a 5lb. tub of vanilla ice cream at a wholesale club and dress it up with all sorts of sundae toppings (homemade or store-bought), such as butterscotch, chocolate, or strawberry syrup; sprinkles; M&Ms; whipped cream; and cherries. You may also want to make or buy pound cake or angel food cake, and serve slices with ice cream and hot sauce or peaches or strawberries.

Garden Parties

The food at a garden party is what you would serve at an afternoon tea, but there's a lot you can do with theme and décor if you have a garden in your backyard.

One woman transformed her garden into "fairyland," with classical music playing, scented candles, and floral wreaths as centerpieces. She researched cooking with edible flowers, such as daisies (but make sure they're organically grown, so that you're not feeding your guests pesticides, that were never meant to be eaten), and served salads of flowers. This idea can be varied by serving fruits and vegetables presented in a flower-like way (radishes and carrots can be crafted into interesting shapes), but this takes research and is time-consuming to carry out. You could also make daisy chains, either as decorations, or as a craft activity with your guests.

Another sample theme for a garden party is a more classical one with games, such as chess, croquet, and horseshoes. You could even ask guests to come in Victorian costume.

You could also transform the garden into a fairground, with makeshift games (ring toss, pie eating contest) and popcorn, cotton candy, Cracker Jacks, and Italian ices, all of which can be bought in bulk.

A well-organized outdoor party on a beautiful summer day can be a truly memorable event for you and your guests. It's usually worth the effort.

Chapter Nine: Odd-Hour Parties

Occasionally, I have found myself in the awkward position of having conflicting entertaining obligations (usually on something like a birthday or Christmas), where I really want to have one side of the family over for "a little something" and I'm not sure how to put it all together. Sometimes I just want to get a few people together, without slaving away in the kitchen, or making a big deal out of it so that they feel no obligation to return the invitation. These are the times when I put together a mid-morning or early afternoon get-together. Other times I just want people to come by for dessert (usually on a Friday evening, when I've worked all day and cooked dinner for myself, and only need to straighten up my home before I entertain) or even just come by for a card game with snacks.

For these odd-hour get-togethers, you must make it clear what food, if any, will be served, and if there is anything you expect your guest to bring.

Breakfast and Brunch

I serve an annual day-after Christmas brunch for my cousins who live in Rhode Island. They drive into the city for Christmas Eve, spend Christmas day with my cousin-in-law's side of the family, and the day after Christmas is the closest we can come to the holiday without causing a scheduling conflict. But I'm exhausted by then (all that shopping and wrapping and cooking and serving), so I don't want to do any more work.

They usually arrive around 11:00 a.m., so the kids have already had a little something to eat. I put out a dozen mixed fresh bagels (you can buy them at wholesale club ahead of time and bagels freeze very well), some whipped cream cheese, which you can dress up by adding cut up olives, scallions, or sun-dried tomatoes, smoked salmon, one sliced purple onion, a large carton of orange juice, and a bottle of Frexinete (a Spanish cava, which is an excellent champagne for mimosas). There's a fresh pot of coffee with creamer and sugar (and Stevia for the non-sugared people), and perhaps some leftover Tsoureki, a Greek sweet bread (that makes a great French toast!), which we eat with tons of whipped butter. I probably have a fruit pie and some sugar cookies left over for dessert.

Quiches are a good choice for brunch food: spinach, broccoli, mushroom, salmon, or a good old Quiche Lorraine.

You can also offer a plate of fresh fruit (sliced cantaloupe and strawberries are available all year round) and cornbread, coffee cake, or a selection of muffins. These baked goods are easy and inexpensive to make with the various mixes on the market or you can buy them cheaply from a wholesale club. Personally, I believe that these are the occasions for which mixes were invented.

If you want to get fancy, you can put out herbed or flavored butter, or a selection of doctored-up cream cheeses and jams (homemade, if you're so inclined). You could also add flavoring for the coffee, as well as cinnamon, maple syrup (one of my friends swears by this in her coffee), and powdered chocolate.

It's hard to serve breakfast to a lot of people because it's a chore to keep eggs warm, unless you use warming trays, which I've never been a big fan of. When I have had more than six people for breakfast, I usually make scrambled eggs with cream cheese, or huevos rancheros (scrambled eggs, a strip of bacon, and shredded cheddar cheese, wrapped in a homemade tortilla and topped with salsa), which I can always warm up in the microwave before serving. However, a Spanish omelet (which is an egg and potato pie) or a fiesta egg scramble (which is really a scrambled egg casserole) would probably make an equally easy and filling breakfast for many.

My father was a great pancake master, and that was his large breakfast food of choice, but I'm just no good at making them. My dad's favorite was blueberry--I'm partial to chocolate chip. You could also serve waffles (which can be bought in quantity at a wholesale club) with fruit, fresh or frozen, and whipped cream. You could also offer fried chicken and waffles with maple syrup and just order the chicken from Popeyes or pick it up at the supermarket the day before, and heat it up.

Sides for breakfast could include either bacon, sausage links, or sliced ham (you can try smoked varieties), all of which you can buy in quantity at a wholesale club. (Check the two-for- one price at a supermarket on bacon or sliced ham—sometimes a supermarket sells it as a buy BOGO free). I cook my bacon in the microwave, which is great for large quantities and no mess. Just place four pieces on a paper towel. Sausage or ham slices however are best prepared in a frying pan on the stove.

Home fried potatoes are cheap and easy to make. Zap potatoes in the microwave until done, peel, and cut them up. Fry them in butter and olive oil with sliced onions and peppers. Toss in a little paprika for garnish. If you like grits or biscuits and gravy, these are also nice additions for breakfast.

Occasionally, I'll have another mother and her kids over for a breakfast play date. Kids feel like it's a treat if you make them farina or fancy oatmeal (add a teaspoon of vanilla and a dash of cinnamon to the mix).

When my son was little his favorite breakfast was green eggs and ham, which I once brought into school for his entire class. You add one drop of green food coloring for every three beaten eggs and scramble in melted butter. For the ham, you add one drop of the food coloring to a melted tablespoon of butter, in which you fry all the ham slices. Kids love this! Another green eggs recipe you can try is deviled eggs; just add food coloring to the yolk/mayonnaise mixture.

While we don't often think about entertaining for breakfast or brunch, it's actually a great time to get together with other working people, and breakfast and brunch are the most casual of the day's meals, so people don't expect as much. Just make sure the coffee is good and hot, the house is clean and cheerful, and the food is fresh and tasty.

Coffee Klatches

Morning get-togethers are a great time to meet with other moms from your kid's school and to really find out what's going on (when the kids aren't there). Most working moms will take a morning off, or go in to work late, to find out what other parents think of the teacher, the school, or the principal. I find people are a lot more honest (and comfortable) in someone's home than at the PTA meeting. The coffee klatch morning meeting is also a good time to have a committee meeting and, if you host it, it's probably cheaper than going out to breakfast, which at today's prices can run $40 per person in New York City.

Even though these early morning coffees are casual (you invite people by asking them when you drop your kids off to school or with a group email), you have to give your guests at least two weeks' warning so that they can rearrange their schedules. Friday mornings seem to be the best time to get together for something like this.

The fare at a coffee klatch is very simple—donuts, coffee, cake, a danish ring (look for those Dunkin Donut, Sarah Lee, or Entenmann's discounts) or bagels and cream cheese. You should offer a pot of tea and both caffeinated and decaffeinated coffee.

The décor for a coffee klatch should also be simple—a nice clean tablecloth, and a centerpiece of flowers or unlit candles. You can use your good china or silver service for the coffee and tea but you don't have to

Afternoon Teas

These can be as casual or as formal as you like—it depends on the occasion and the host.

A baby or engagement shower could be an afternoon tea, in which case it would be much more formal (by Evite or even a mailed invitation), with matching china, tea cups, and a silver tea service, which you should be able to pick up at a flea market or church bazaar (don't be afraid to negotiate for this).

You should also have a lace or linen tablecloth, and you might want to have linen napkins (or at least the fancy beverage napkins). This is the time to use those napkin holders you've been given as presents, or you can make some out of gold foil or thick, pastel ribbons (simple and elegant). This is also the time to use those paper doilies under the platters, if they are to your liking.

The food for an afternoon tea can be very simple—from tea sandwiches (white bread, with the crust removed, stuffed with a selection of egg salad, chicken salad, cucumber and cream cheese, or olives and cream cheese on raisin bread, and cut into quarters) to the more elaborate, such as scones, ladyfingers, sugar, cookies, mini cheesecakes, etc.

Make sure you have enough sugar, and Stevia, sliced lemons, and honey, and put out cream, as well as low fat, and possibly oat and/or Lactaid milk. You will probably need more than one sugar and creamer bowl set, and you can mix and match these, but try to keep them in the same color scheme. You may also want to put out a few different pots of tea—an Earl Grey, a mint, and perhaps something with a fruit base. You could put these on the table in teapots of very different patterns—no one will expect you to have matching tea pots.

Every year I visit the Jordan Pond restaurant in Acadia National Park in Bar Harbor, Maine, and have afternoon tea outdoors, overlooking a lake. They serve hot popovers with strawberry jam that are out of this world. For a group of 12 or less, popovers are wonderful, and pretty easy to make. You just have to refrigerate the batter the night before and bake them in muffin pans.

If you're having a very formal tea, where you really want to impress or entertain your guests, you might want to hire a teenager to pour the tea and serve the tea sandwiches. They would wear serving attire, and you could ask them to wear gloves for a special effect.

Dessert Parties

I like having people over for dessert, usually around 7:00 p.m. if there are children coming.

As with breakfast and coffee klatches, I make sure everyone knows I'm just serving coffee and dessert. If it's a workday, I might ask each family to bring something. This way I have more variety to offer.

As usual, I'd like to make a pie (typically apple, because I'll buy bags of apples on a regular basis, so I always have some on hand) and cookies or brownies. I would make both coffee and tea.

If I was feeling particularly festive, I might buy some coffee flavorings (hazelnut, chocolate raspberry, vanilla—although you can make them yourself, if you have time), or by one or two of those creamers with flavors (Irish cream, amaretto, French vanilla). I might also put out a selection of after dinner cordials (we always have some Bailey's Irish Cream, Kahlúa, and Cointreau) to add to the coffee, as well as whipped cream. Cinnamon sticks, or chocolate, covered stirred add a nice touch.

A family member makes a wonderful flan (a Latin custard dessert), which she would often bring. Rice pudding also goes extremely well this time of year, as does a homemade trifle, (a sort of kitchen sink dessert that's great when you have a little bit of everything left over). I also found a recipe for a sort of homemade ice cream cake (a layer of mashed graham crackers, Kahlúa and rum, coffee ice cream, mashed up macaroons, chocolate shavings, and frozen whipped cream) that's very fancy and impressive, and easy, so I might serve that. It takes about 20 minutes to make and you have to freeze it for two hours before serving.

You can make your dessert gathering even fancier if you have a cappuccino machine, or you might borrow one. Espresso is easy to make with a greca, which is a stainless steel two piece coffee pot you heat on the stove. You can pick one up fairly inexpensively in hardware stores and some department stores. Add lots of sugar and lemon peel, and hot milk or cream. You might be able to pick up a set of demitasse cups at a rummage sale or buy a set for about $10 at the housewares outlet.

Card Games and Game Nights

I used to be in a weekly poker game that started around 8:00 p.m. and ended at around 11:30. Many of the people came after work and were supposed to have eaten, but hadn't, so the snacks we had were important. We took a contribution from each player of something like $5 each, but the person who was hosting was supposed to have the food and beverages there when we arrived.

Each host was also responsible for poker chips (at least 200 for five players) and cards, which cost a bundle if you have to run out and buy them at the last minute, but which can be found at any dollar store if you plan ahead (sometimes you can get two decks of cards for as little as a dollar). You can also find poker chips at thrift shops.

When one of the guys hosted, we usually just had the standard potato chips, canned dip, pretzels, peanuts, and beer fare. However, they loved it when I would put out a bowl of guacamole, homemade popcorn, a soup mix dip with veggie sticks, and, if I was feeling particularly creative, a zapped batch of nachos. A box of heated up frozen appetizers from a wholesale club (jalapeño poppers, pigs in a blanket) were always a big hit.

To stretch the dollar on the drinks, I often made a pitcher of iced tea instead of serving soda (everyone seems to like this). Beer is a staple at these games, so I usually buy two six-packs (one light beer, one regular). I invested in a Soda Stream machine, so I always have seltzer as well. I always make sure I empty my ice trays into a large bowl in the freezer and refill them before the players arrive.

More and more of my friends have invited me over for casual game nights of Cards Against Humanity or even old favorites like Monopoly,

Trivial Pursuit, Pictionary, etc. Some of these game nights have started with pizza and then gone on to the game afterwards. Occasionally we get together to watch a classic film, or watch the first film in a series, and then go out and see the new film together.

I know many people get together on a regular basis to play Dungeons & Dragons or Masquerade. I like to imagine that those players create snacks and beverages that are fantasy-related and coincide with the game, like mulled wine and some sort of dragon tacos. I am sure there's a D & D cookbook to inspire.

Odd-hour parties can be a challenge, but they can also be fun and warm in a more casual way than the full scale lunches, and dinners. And if you host a regular card game or game night, it's a really nice way to see your friends on a regular basis. For the poker game, it floated from house to house, and that made it even nicer because no one had to do all the work.

Chapter Ten: Children's Birthday Parties

Anyone who has ever thrown a few kids parties, or gone to a few hundred parties for kids, or has more than one child in their family, knows how expensive these parties can be—and how important they are to your child.

I truly admire Amy Dacyczyn for throwing her son an amazing pirate party, described in the first volume of *The Tightwad Gazette* for something like $10 in 1992. It's inspiring to know it can be done! While I don't think I'll ever manage to get away with a children's party that cheaply, I made a personal vow that my son's birthday parties would not be more expensive than a family weekend in Washington DC. With a lot of thought and ingenuity and hard work, I've managed to throw better kids parties and save myself a bundle.

Kids parties break down into a couple of categories—at home (indoors or outdoors), in a rented space, or at an entertainment facility. They also break down into age groups because you can't throw the same kind of party for a toddler as a preteen or teenager.

The Basic At-Home Kids' Party

If you're having a kids' party at home, whether the child is three or 13, there is a basic shape to the party. You should have between six and 20 kid guests (more than that will be hard to accommodate indoors), usually for lunch, but sometimes for an early dinner. Friday evenings seem to be more and more popular for kids' parties.

The meal should be kid-friendly and can be anything from hotdogs, pizza, or chicken tenders, to even peanut butter and jelly sandwiches. If you're making a barbecue, kids love burgers, ribs, or chicken. Fried mozzarella sticks with marinara sauce are a nice treat, and you can buy them in bulk at a wholesale club.

It's tempting to go with juice boxes for drinks because they're easy but they're expensive. Better to offer jugs of juice and soda, or make lemonade, iced tea, or root beer floats, which are favorites from my own childhood. I like to serve egg creams and milkshakes, and ice cream sodas, which are terrific kid pleasers.

The choice of cake should be up to your child: an ice cream cake; a sheet cake from a bakery; a special themed cake with a homemade filling or frosting; cupcakes, which the kids can decorate themselves; or ice cream sundaes. My son really likes Reese's peanut butter cups so I've made a number of Reese's peanut butter cup chocolate cakes for his birthday with no complaints from his friends.

You should have balloons around the house, as well as streamers, and Happy Birthday signs and murals, which can be homemade. You can even have the guests help decorate a commemorative mural, using a white tablecloth or packing paper taped to the wall and asking each guest to contribute.

For a young child, hats, and a birthday tablecloth on the table are de rigueur. I'd like to have themed tableware, but you could use just plain paper cups, plates, and napkins. You can also have the kids make their own hats out of newspaper or construction paper. This is especially fun for princess themed parties!

Children's birthday parties last between two and three hours. You need some sort of entertainment, whether it's party games with prizes (the old standards are pin the tail on the donkey, musical chairs, hot potato, pass the parcel, charades, bean toss, etc.), a movie, watching a sporting event (for slightly older kids), paid entertainment, arts, and crafts, dancing, karaoke, or limbo. Girls sometimes have makeover parties, at home or at a beauty parlor.

I love piñata's, for children of all ages. You can vary what you fill it with for the different ages of the children, but all kids love bashing at a swaying target, and then diving for candy and prizes.

For a birthday party for a child under 10, I believe in goody bags for the guests. Many kids open their presents in front of their guests, and it's hard for a kid not to feel a little jealous. Goody bags take the sting out. You don't have to fill it with outrageously expensive things, just candy and snacks, and a few choice items from the dollar store.

While a kids' party can cost as little as $100, that's not realistic for me with my working urban life. I'd say a themed party for 10 kids is going to run at least $200 (including coffee and cake for any adults who want to hang around). This budget makes me feel that I can be creative, but without overspending. It's also about what I budget for most of my at home adult parties.

About three months before the child's birthday, I start casing the dollar stores, Odd Lots, and party outlet stores to see what themes are on sale. I can begin presenting my child with options for the party theme. Kids tend to have fairly basic theme ideas, so it's not hard to match your child's wishes with what you could afford, or to make them think it was their idea to have a Marvel party when you thought of it because you saw the Marvel party stuff for 50% off.

Once your kid has chosen a theme, you can go through all the party elements (hats, tableware, goody bags, games, or entertainment, music, food, cake), and see how you can tailor each one to the theme. Some of the themes might have websites where you can go for ideas (such as Disney and Universal), and some might even have forums where you can get feedback from other parents and kids.

You can send the party invitations out with Evites, especially if you're inviting your child's whole class as well as relatives.

You still must send out thank you notes to those who attended, as well as those who sent a gift without coming. You can do this via email, but written notes are so nice, and you might want to do this with your child so that they learn this skill. You should send the thank you notes no later than 10 days after the party. These too can be homemade, and are actually sweeter if they're designed and written by the child.

How to Make a Piñata

Sometimes, if you're really lucky, a piñata that goes with your child's theme or generic birthday party (rainbow, birthday cake) is on super sale. If you live near the Mexican border, you might be able to get one really cheaply in a border town. However, it's just as easy to make them, and a lot more fun for you and your child.

A piñata is easy to make, but you have to start it a few days before you need it. Blow up a balloon (this will give you a circular or tubular shape to start with) and cover it with newspaper strips generously dipped in a paste made of equal amounts (usually about 2 ½ cups each) of flour and water. For the average piñata, you'll need between 20 and 30 one-inch wide strips of newspaper. To make a figure, add empty toilet paper and paper towel rolls for arms and legs or necks and beaks. Attach them to the balloon with masking tape, then cover with the newspaper strips. Finish shaping the piñata to your heart's desire.

Let the piñata dry overnight, and pop the balloon with a pin. The empty space is where the candy and prizes go.

Paint the outside of the piñata with acrylic paint (you can pick up the four primary collars cheaply, so don't bother mixing paint together for this) and decorate. Let the paint dry overnight. Add extras to the piñata the next day, such as tissue paper, glitter, buttons, etc. Also attach a bobby pin or paper clip somewhere on the piñata, so you have a place to tie the string when you hang it. You also have to carve a small circular hole in the back of the piñata through which you can add the candy. You can tape the hole up again when the piñata is full.

The easiest piñatas to make are the superheroes (capes made out of tissue paper, which you can also pick up at the dollar store), Mickey Mouse's head, animals, dinosaurs, and dinosaur eggs, etc. Use your imagination, and you should be able to come up with a simplified version of the piñata of your child's dreams, using basic shapes (circular torsos made from balloons, arms and legs from paper rolls, beaks and necks from rolled up oak tag or cardboard or construction paper). You can also go online for inspiration, and how to YouTube videos.

If you child insists on a difficult piñata, (castle, a pirate ship) and you can't talk them into a simpler one associated with the theme, (a knight, a pirate chest), then you may have to buy one, but they can run anywhere from $25-$75 at a party store). However, you may be able to find an artist on Etsy or online who would make something like this for you cheaper.

Filling the piñata is easy too. Buy dollar store bags of individually wrapped candy and gum, such as Bazooka, peanut butter cups, lifesaver packs, chocolate bars, tootsie rolls, and lollipops, as well as a few more impressive items, such as ring pops, wax lips (a personal favorite), giant sweet tarts, whistles, erasers, candy necklaces, small cards, stickers, etc. Most party and dollar stores have a party section where they offer packages of six or eight prizes. This is definitely where you should be looking for piñata filling, although I have seen a bag of candy and treats sold as piñata filling. If you had odd pieces left over from the goody bags, you can put them in here too. You should also check what the online stores Archie McPhee, and Oriental Trading have to offer.

Use a child's baseball bat or broomstick to swap the piñata. If you have really young kids, you might have to "start" the opening, but do that after each kid has taken a turn.

Making Up Goody Bags

Unless you run yourself ragged, these will cost between $3 and $5 per bag. Some people can do it for less, but I would lose my mind trying.

You do not have to buy fancy goody bags. Most kids are so eager to see what's inside, they don't even notice that you went to the trouble of getting officially licensed *Star Wars* bags (which can cost a pretty penny). Of course, if they're on sale and absolutely precious, you might consider it, but it's more for you than for the kids.

It is easy to make your own party bags. Use either brown lunch bags or white bakery bags and do some simple art on the bags to go with the party. It could be as simple as writing "Happy Birthday" or "Goody Bag" in glitter on the bag. One mom hosted a *101 Dalmatians* party and bought a rubberstamp of dog paw prints, which were stamped on brown bags. You can buy stickers of the theme and plaster them on the bags or stencil bags with pictures related to the theme. Simple and easy is the key.

You can also have goody bags along seasonal themes, such as back to school, Halloween, Christmas, and summer vacation.

The back to school goody bags featured school carry cases with pencils, erasers, pencil sharpeners, rulers, and notepads. You can get these at a dollar store. The case is the goody bag.

For Halloween goody bags, you can make a white bag into a ghost or buy trick-or-treat bags (which should be fairly inexpensive), and use these. You should be able to buy such things as bat or ant rings, eyeball chocolates, Halloween magnets, wax lips with fangs, face painting kits, fangs, fake fingertips, press on tattoos, and plastic bugs and snakes to put in the bags

For Christmas goody bags, you can wrap a ribbon around the bag so that it looks like a present or make your own bags out of cheap wrapping paper. You could put in Christmas magnets, red and green foil, covered chocolates, and candy canes. You can have the kids make ornaments at the party, and use these as part of the goody bag as well.

Summer goody bags include bottles of bubbles, sidewalk chalk, and water guns. Kids love these.

I try to put four items in each goody bag, and about four pieces of candy and/or snack food, unless I give each kid one bigger present.

Miscellaneous items for goody bags, many of which can be purchased in packs of six or eight or ordered in bulk from a party or teacher catalog, are: whistles, stickers, tattoos, crayon packs, bubbles, erasers, water guns, whoopee cushions and other gag novelties, mini puzzles, watercolor paint kits, pencils, decorative pens, magic markers, clay, silly putty, Slinkys, bouncing balls, paddles with balls, jacks, cars, fake make up for girls, lipgloss, kids' sunglasses, kids' disguise glasses, and various pop culture items of the moment (KPop, Taylor Swift, etc.).

I don't like to fill goody bags with candy, because as a mother I don't like my child coming home all excited from a party, and then bouncing off the walls for a few hours from all the candy. I usually include one or two pieces of candy such as a tootsie pop, some gum, and then snack foods like fruit roll-ups, bags of peanuts, rice crispy treats, raisins, etc.

Another mom waited until she knew exactly who was coming (she sent the invitations out very early) and ordered individual stampers with each kid's name on it. She added stamp pads and some treats, and the bags probably ran her about $5 per kid,. This was quite thoughtful and creative.

Kids' Games

We all assume that everyone knows the standard children's games, but there are always one or two that are unfamiliar to someone. For instance, I never played pass the parcel at parties when I was a kid.

Since games are competitive, you might want to have small prizes for the kids to win. They should be different from what you put in the goody bags. I usually buy three or four special toys at the dollar store, such as a puzzle, action figure, or Barbie-type of doll clothing for the girls or some kind of book.

Musical Chairs: Count the number of kids and have one chair less than the number. Arrange the chairs in a line or circle, and place a kid in front of each chair. Leave a space for the chair that is "missing." When the kids are in place, play music, and have the kids walk around the circle or around the line of chairs. When the music is stopped, the kids scramble for seats. The kid left without a seat loses that round, and a chair is removed. You do this until there is only one chair and two kids left. The kid sitting in the chair at the end wins the round.

Hot Potato: Same concept as musical chairs. The kids sit in a circle and pass a ball (one mother actually used a potato wrapped in aluminum foil) around the circle (pretending it's hot), accompanied by music. When the music stops abruptly, whoever is holding the ball loses that round. The last kid left without the ball wins.

Pass the Parcel: This concept is similar to hot potato, but with a twist. The kids sit in a circle and a gift-wrapped box is passed around. When the music stops, whoever is holding the parcel unwraps one layer. There's usually four or five layers of wrapping, so the kid unwrapping the present on the last stop gets to keep the present inside. You can do this a couple of times.

Pin the Tail on the Donkey: A drawing of a donkey (or any other animal you want, or some person or creature that goes with your birthday theme) is taped to a wall. Each kid is given a tail with tape, blindfolded, spun around a couple of times, so that they lose their bearings, and then let loose to hopefully pin the tail on the donkey in the right place. However, the kids are usually way off base and end up pinning the tail on the donkey's nose or knees, which makes for lots of laughs. The kid whose tail lands closest to where the tail is supposed to be wins this game.

Bean Toss: Using a cardboard box, you make a target of some sort (usually pretty big and round, so the kids have a chance of getting it in) and give them three to five bean bags that they toss at the target. The kid who gets the most bull's eyes wins.

Charades: This is for slightly older kids (five and up) because they have to work as a team. Divide the kids into teams of three, four, or five, and have them pick clues that you made up ahead of time related to movies, books, or characters a kid would know, or to the theme of the party.

One kid on each team picks a clue from a bowl or hat, and has two or three minutes (use a timer) to pantomime it for the other kids on their team, so that they guess what it is. If the time runs out before they have guessed correctly, they lose the round, and the other teams can guess at the clue. Whichever team has the most correct answers wins, and you give prizes to all that team's members.

Pictionary: For Pictionary, you need an easel with large paper on which the kids draw clues for their teammates. They pick a clue out of the hat, and then must illustrate the clue, either as a word, or in syllables, in a given time.

This is by no means a complete list of games to play at kids' parties, but these are the most common ones. You can also have a treasure hunt, which involves hiding items around the house or backyard. A limbo contest can be lots of fun, but you have to find a way to set up a broom horizontally about four feet off the ground and then be able to lower it little by little. Kids have to shimmy under the broom without touching it or be disqualified. The broom is lowered slightly after each round. The last child standing is the winner. Another game is to have all the kids try to keep a balloon up in the air by batting it around volleyball style. Whoever lets the balloon touch the ground is out.

Themes for Parties

Creating a well-thought-out theme party is easy, it just takes time and creativity. The goal of a child's birthday party should be to make a child's fantasies come true for a day.

Choose a theme for your child's party based on their favorite movies, TV shows, and hobbies. Before you approach your child with your ideas, give each one a little thought yourself, so you have some basic ideas on how you can put it all together.

Indiana Jones. One year I threw an Indiana Jones party for my son. I sent out photocopied black-and-white invitations with a picture of Harrison Ford in his Doctor Jones gear, inviting my sons' friends to a reception to honor Dr. Jones after his return from the Amazon.

We decided to re-create the banquet in *Indiana Jones and the Temple of Doom,* which consisted of eyeball soup, rhino beetles, snake surprise, and chilled monkey brains. I made tomato soup with floating ping-pong balls for eyeballs, which was a big hit with the kids, and they each got to take eyeball ping-pong balls home. I found plastic rhino beetles at the party store and put one on each slice of pizza I served the kids. I photo-copied a simple drawing of a monkey's head and glued it to the outside of a paper cup and served orange and raspberry swirl sherbet as the chilled monkey brains. A homemade chocolate cake with candy worms, and snakes, arranged to spell out "Happy Birthday" was the snake surprise.

For the activities, we had a treasure hunt in the park outside our building. The treasure was a gold plastic Ferraro chocolate box crammed with fake coins and dollar bills, necklaces, rings, and charms. We made a map of the park and gave each kid a piece of it, which they had to put together to find the treasure. We also glued or taped plastic spiders, bugs, snakes, and mice onto the playground equipment, and the kids put these in their goody bags when they found them.

After the treasure hunt, we had them smack a spider piñata, which I was lucky enough to find for $10. I filled it with skull and bat rings, necklaces, and candy that I bought in a variety pack.

I was lucky enough to find plastic "gangster" hats (fedoras) in the party store for $.79 each at that time. The found candy and plastic bugs and the hat where the kids party favors.

I had intended to use a plain white paper tablecloth with a hand-drawn treasure map as the table covering, but I was lucky enough to find a set of tableware with an insect motif at 50% off at the local party store. The tablecloth was plastic, which was an added bonus.

Princess Party: This is a universal party theme for girls, ages 3 to 12.

One mother created a princess party by buying a whole bunch of party and prom dresses at rummage sales before her daughter's birthday. She let the girls add glitter and sequins and jeweled buttons and sashes. She also bought a ton of rummage sale costume jewelry for them to wear. Princess hats were made out of oak tag, covered with material with a rummage sale scarf thrust through the hole in the top to hang down the back.

Lunch was an elegant tea party with sandwiches and cake. You could also feature a light fare such as quiche or crêpes.

Better than any goody bag, each girl got to take home her princess costume. If you still wanted to include goody bags, great choices would be generic necklaces, rings, makeup, false nails, tiaras, and glass slippers (which I once found at a party store for 34 cents many years ago.)

Medieval Times: The first thing I would do is re-create the meal they serve at the Medieval Times restaurant—garlic bread, vegetable soup, that's drunk directly out of a bowl, chicken, ribs, and roasted potatoes eaten with your hands (which kids love). I'd serve soda or apple cider in plastic beer mugs, and cupcakes, which are also easily eaten with your hands.

Each kid would make their own tunic (just pre-cut felt and hot glue), as well as a coat of arms on a shield (white oak tag on cardboard with a strap glued on). You could also try making armor out of cardboard covered in aluminum foil.

For games, I might have an archery contest of some sort of Nerf-like bow with rubber stick-on arrows, and some variation of Hot Potato (Hot Grail), and musical chairs with Gregorian chants. Maybe a Pin the Tail on the Armored Horse or Pin the Horn on the Unicorn or a Pin the Fire on the Dragon.

I would want to give each child a plastic sword or axe with their goody bag, but I would check with the moms first. Some moms are dead set against their children having weapons, and I wouldn't want to make anyone uncomfortable.

Pirate: As I mentioned, I was so impressed with Amy' Dacyczyn's brilliant pirate party in the first volume of *The Tightwad Gazette*, and that's as cheap as it gets. She built a pirate ship in a barn out of old sheets and odds and ends. The kids also had a treasure hunt with clues that lead to a treasure box with 300 chocolate covered coins, which the kids split for their goody bag loot.

The food consisted of generic soda and ice cream, and a sheet cake with the treasure map on it. Dacyczyn reported that the party cost less than $10 (but that was close to 40 years ago). However, this is clearly the kind of party that requires a basement or backyard (or rental space).

An indoor party can be done by making pirate costumes for all the kids (eyepatches, bandannas, pirate hats—black felt or newspaper hats). Maybe let the kids make their own pirate flags? The treasure hunt with chocolate coins is the perfect activity for a pirate party. I might have the kids make their own swords out of two crossed pieces of cardboard or wood or I might supply plastic swords in the goody bags.

The pirate party theme can be easily adapted into a Peter Pan party, if that is one of your child's favorite films or stories.

Movie Star: You'll need lots of rummage sale clothing (men's suits and gowns), lots of makeup and hair styling items, and lots of sunglasses, feather boas, wild hats, and glittery jewelry.

One mother put up a sheet on the wall and took pictures of all the kids in their movie star get up. She had multiple prints made of the pictures, and then gave the guests picture books as their souvenir for the party.

If you know of a shop that sells old magazines, try to negotiate a good price and get some back issues of old movie star magazines. And give them out as souvenirs. The kids will be fascinated by these, as they did not grow up with them.

You can make placemats out of cut-outs from magazines or you could draw a Hollywood star out of gold glitter on each place setting and write the guest's name on it.

You could do a similar thing with the sheet cake. Using white frosting on the cake, make a large star in the center with the birthday child's name, and then try smaller stars with the guest's names around it in another color frosting.

Dinosaur: This kind of party is a big favorite for younger kids. You can call it a *Jurassic Park* party or just a dinosaur dig.

Kids love a dinosaur dig, which you can have in the backyard (you can buy bones or make your own fossils with plaster of paris molds or just make a bone mold). You can also have a dinosaur egg hunt, using those plastic Easter eggs (put a tiny plastic dinosaur inside each egg). You could also play Hot Dinosaur Egg, a variation on the Hot Potato game.

You can make that exploding volcano cake (look up the recipe on YouTube) and put plastic dinosaurs on the icing.

There are lots of arts and crafts possibilities with this theme. You can tape white paper to the walls and ask the kids to draw or paint a mural like the ones they've see in the museums. We bought dinosaur molds a natural history museum. If you make dinosaurs from the plaster of paris molds, the kids can paint them at the party and take the painted dinosaurs home as souvenirs.

For the tablecloth, you could put each kid's place setting in a giant dinosaur footprint. A dinosaur piñata will be easy to make (most likely candidates for this are brontosaurus and stegosaurus) and easy to fill. Same for the goody bags, which you could make out of brown paper bags with dinosaur foot prints stamped on them and filled with plastic dinosaurs, dinosaur stickers, chocolate covered "dinosaur eggs, etc.

Goosebumps/Wednesday/Haunted House: This is really a Halloween party any time of the year, and it's pretty easy to find horror-related kid's stuff at a fraction of the cost after Halloween. Encourage the kids to come in costume. You could serve a witch's brew. The cake could be decorated to look like a graveyard.

Party games could be a blast; dunk for apples; turn your home into a haunted house with cobwebs and funny scary gags throughout (look up Halloween decorations). Blindfold the kids and have them place their hands in bowls filled with stuff that will gross them out… but thrill them when they see what it really is! Have them put their hands in a bowl of water and spaghetti and tell them it's brains; have them hold a peeled, very lightly boiled egg, which you tell them is an eyeball; and put some wet dough in a plastic bag and tell them it's someone's liver. Kids love this kind of stuff! Don't forget to play scary music.

Since I'm pretty well stocked with Halloween decorations, I would probably use my Halloween tablecloth, cookie jar, candlesticks, etc. For a meal in winter, I might make pumpkin beef stew (beef stew served inside a jack-o'-lantern) or jack-o'-lantern shaped pasta.

For the goody bags, in addition to all the fangs and spiders you can put in the bags, you could put in horror tattoos and books. FiveBelow often has horror coloring books.

Superheroes: This is a fairly easy party to put together because most of the items can be bought inexpensively. There have been so many Marvel and DC movies in the last decade that you should be able to pick up all sorts of party favors and decorations at a super discount. You can also buy superhero figurines and put them on the cake in the icing. You're also likely to find a superhero piñata for a good price, although they are easy to make.

If you are extremely generous and handy with a sewing machine, you could easily whip up a half dozen or so superhero capes (with cotton material from a discount store, and a felt insignia). The kids would love you forever!

Space/Aliens: Astronauts and aliens are always kid favorites, so it should be pretty easy to put together a space/aliens party. The piñata could be in the shape of a spacecraft or a planet or an alien head, filled with NASA-like figurines (they sell them in packages like toy soldiers now), alien erasers, alien lollipops, "moon" rocks, etc.

You can decorate your house with the solar system, either homemade cut-outs or mini piñata planets. NASA will send you packets of information and posters for the cost of postage if you email them, and you could put some of these in the goody bags and use others as decorations. You can play Pin the Planet on the Solar System, Hot Sun, Planet Toss, etc.

You can serve Tang with the birthday lunch. You can also buy space ice cream or a cake in the shape of a spacecraft, or decorate a sheet cake with the solar system.

Arts and Crafts: This is for kids who love to create things. You can do anything from ceramic molds (premade) to tie-dying and T-shirt decorating (with glitter glue or special T-shirt paint), as well as making ornaments for Christmas. You can also have the kids make those small Legos projects that feature everything from Godzilla monsters to flowers.

In general, you have to be extremely well-prepared for these kind of parties with kids (picture glue in the hair and paint on your rugs and floor) but they can be a lot of fun, especially when the kid has a momento made by themselves to remind them of the party.

You can easily fill goody bags with art supplies. I've seen watercolor sets, pastels, glitter glue, packages of paint brushes, and all sorts of art supplies for sale in bulk at dollar stores. You can also buy a lot of the stuff at party stores or through craft catalogs or general merchandise catalogs.

Alice in Wonderland/Through the Looking Glass: A friend turned her living room into Alice's Wonderland for daughter's sixth birthday. She copied the illustrations from the Tennille edition of the book, had a Mad Tea party lunch, played indoor croquet, and had the girls make houses of cards. For the goody bag, she gave out little porcelain tea sets that she'd picked up at the dollar store, mini editions of the book, and a deck of cards so the girls could make their own house of cards at home.

Dr. Seuss: A Dr. Seuss party is great for young kids, ages three to six. The Children's Museum of Manhattan had a Dr. Seuss exhibit when my son was younger, so many of these ideas were inspired by that exhibit. There is also a Dr. Seuss website which has a wealth of games and ideas for you as well.

There's a lot you can do with the Cat in the Hat motif, such as hiding a number of pink dots (made of pink felt or construction paper) throughout the home for the kids to find and "clean," like in *The Cat in the Hat Comes Back,* with brooms and feather dusters. You could also have each child make a Cat in the Hat hat (oak tag stove pipe hats) that you let the kids decorate themselves.

The cake can be either a Cat in the Hat-shaped hat or a sheet cake decorated to look like the cover of your child's favorite Dr. Seuss book. Consider serving strawberry-flavored Quick with straws as the pink ink the Zink drinks. A Dr. Suess party can be a blast.

Winnie the Pooh: The same friend of mine who transformed her house in Wonderland also, on the occasion of her four-year old daughter's birthday, turned the house into the Hundred Acre Wood. She made her own Winnie the Pooh decorations for the walls (Rabbit's house in one corner, Owl's in another, etc.) And made newspaper hats for the kids (a la Christopher Robin). For the party game she hid real carrots throughout the apartment (with their greens) and the kid who found the most carrots won a prize, which was somehow Pooh-related, such as stickers or pens. There was a Pooh cake and Pooh related stuff in the goody bags.

Disney movies tend to have a lot of tie-in opportunities so definitely visit the websites for ideas for games and recipes. You can do the same for almost any popular children's movie or TV show.

Teen Parties and Slumber Parties

When kids get a little older, they sometimes get more demanding and generic birthday parties often are just not enough. A little ingenuity can go along way here.

Teenager parties have changed since my son was young. You can simply have the kids over to watch a sporting event or a movie (or series) or just to play games and feed them.

For girls, you can often have a make-up or manicure party or hairstyling night. You could even have a night where everyone changes their hair color to a color not found in nature that can be washed out (but ask the moms first). If you have a friend who is particularly good at this, now is the time to ask for a favor.

One family served a fancy five-course meal chosen by the birthday girl. The mom and dad dressed up as a chef and a maître d' for the night. You can also have a number of kids over for a cooking party. Let the birthday kid pick out the menu. Each kid could receive a copy of the recipes and photos of them cooking as mementos.

When kids are older, it's easier because they know exactly what they want. You could order in Chinese food with fortune cookies or Japanese sushi. It's up to you and your child.

If your kids are creative, you might want to have sewing party. I used to get together with my friends to make jean skirts when I was a teenager. We would make maxi skirts from old jeans and sew triangles of tapestries or velvet material between the pant legs. You can also have an arts and crafts party with the teenagers.

You can easily make any of these teen parties into a slumber party (have the kids bring sleeping bags or make bed rolls) but the number of guests should be no more than six or seven (and make sure you have all the parents' phone numbers and know what each child is allergic to). In addition to a crafts or make up session, you can rent videos and serve an exotic breakfast in the morning or take them all out to breakfast.

Mad Libs are quite fun at parties. You fill in the blanks of a poem, story, or essay, so that it comes out funny— "Four score and seven ----- ago," etc. I believe they still sell these but you could easily make them for yourself.

Truth or Dare, where you ask each other embarrassing questions and choose whether to answer or take a dare, is still a popular way for kids to have some good laughs together. They might also want to play Magic Eight

Ball where you ask the supposedly magic ball questions about your future and it answers yes, no, or maybe. I also remember having lots of tarot readings and playing with the Ouija Board at some of these parties (although there are parents who may not approve of this, so ask first). If you are so inclined, you might consider dressing up as a fortune teller and reading the girl's fortunes. You can bone up on this online before the party.

Renting Space

Renting space could run between $200 and $500, but it really will ease your mind for cleanup and survival of your rugs, walls, and furniture. If you're having more than 20 kids and their parents, and you don't have a backyard or big house, you might also want to consider this, especially because the space will come with parking.

As I mentioned earlier, you can usually find space to rent in a co-op or condo building, the local community center, or even a health club (one little girl's parents had an exercise party there, complete with a trainer). You might also want to consider renting space if you are going to be having a particularly messy arts and crafts party or food-related event, or if your party theme will have a number of big games (such as a circus or carnival theme).

Many parents hold their party at a children's entertainment facility, such as a Chuck E. Cheese or a fast food chain, but they're all expensive and not very personal.

Birthday Entertainment and Help

If you decide to have a home party and want to supply the entertainment, there are a number of options. Of course this could run you hundreds of dollars.

Reach out to the local community center where your child might already be taking classes. There might be a teacher who might be interested in supplying a half hour to an hour's worth of instruction or entertainment for a bunch of kids. This usually include people who teach music or art to youngsters (we have a musical munchkins for woman who teaches kids songs, plays guitar, and brings a bag of triangles, maracas, and tambourines for the kids to play along). The art teacher can guide the kids in making birthday hats or mementos. If you have a backyard, or access to a gym, the local coach might be persuaded to giving kids basic tips on basketball, soccer or baseball, depending on the time of year.

Traditional staples of at-home entertainment include clowns and magicians, but one variation on this theme is to have the clown or the magician teach the kids how to do the tricks or pratfalls. Kids would remember this more than the average party. You could then put simple tricks or gags in your goody bags.

Planning a complicated craft project for them kids such as glitter glue T-shirts for five-year-olds, you might want to hire a teenager to act as an extra set of party ends. You could probably also use the help in getting the food from the kitchen to the kids and back again, if you're having a large number of kids and their parents don't stay. Can also help with cleaning up after the party is over. You have to pay teenagers at least minimum wage, that's $15 an hour is probably a fair amount.

You could also have an artist paint the kids' faces around your theme (or do it yourself). I've seen some wonderful designs for superhero face painting. Check out YouTube videos and see what options there are. I'm told that if you mix acrylic paint with dish soap, it is very easy to wash off.

There are alternatives to clowns and magicians at children's parties as well, from people who do balloon art to theatrical plays featuring your child's favorite character. There are jugglers (and those who will teach your kids to juggle and you can then give out balls with the goody bags), puppet shows, artists, etc.

The best way to find entertainment for parties is through word of mouth, or through some kind of neighborhood directories such as NextDoor or even your local Facebook listing. You might be able to hire students such as beauty school students, local music students, artists, etc. It should not cost you more than $200 to hire entertainment for an hour unless the supplies for what they are teaching are very expensive.

Birthday parties for children and teens are really important to your child's memories of self and family, as well as those of their peers. There are certain parties and gatherings I remember from my childhood that inspired me to go the extra mile for my own child. I truly believe that all it really takes is the desire to do something really special that you know your child will appreciate, and taking the time to be as creative as you possibly can be.

About the Author

Lori Perkins is a veteran literary agent, publisher, and author based in New York City, known for her practical "frugal writing" approach to creating and publishing books. With more than 35 years in the publishing industry, she has built a reputation for producing smart, timely content while avoiding the bloated budgets and slow timelines of traditional publishing.

As founder of the **L. Perkins Agency** and CEO of **Riverdale Avenue Books**, Perkins has championed a digital-first publishing model that emphasizes efficiency, low overhead, and maximizing the value of every idea.

Perkins is also known as an **anthology specialist**, having edited more than 25 collections that bring together diverse voices on timely topics—from *Fifty Writers on Fifty Shades of Grey* to *1984 in the 21st Century*. Her collaborative approach reflects her belief that great publishing doesn't have to be expensive—it just has to be smart.

In addition to her work as an agent and publisher, Perkins is the author of **The Insider's Guide to Getting an Agent** (Writer's Digest Books) and the frugal entertaining classic **How to Throw Fabulous Parties on a Budget**. She is currently working on **La Vida Broka: How to Live Richly When You're Dirt Poor**, co-written with Angela Torres.

A former journalism instructor at New York University and a longtime contributor to industry publications, Perkins frequently shares her insights on writing, publishing, and creative efficiency.

A breast cancer survivor, she also leads a free monthly online workshop, **Healing Through Journaling**, through the Dubin Breast Center at Mount Sinai, and hosts free Zoom journaling sessions for creative writers through Riverdale Senior Services.

Through her work as an author, teacher, and publisher, Lori Perkins continues to champion the idea that creativity thrives not on lavish budgets, but on resourcefulness, collaboration, and imagination.

Visit her website at LoriPerkins.net

Other Books by Lori Perkins

La Vida Broka: How to Live Richly When You're Dirt Poor
with Angela Torres

Hungry for Your Love

Still Hungry for Your Love

The Book of Everyday Resistance

1984 in the 21st Century: An Anthology of Essays

MeToo! Essays About How and Why This Happened, What It Means and How to Make Sure It Never Happens Again

Fifty Writers on Fifty Shades of Grey

Two Dukes are Better Than One as Lorna James

Two Dukes and a Lady as Lorna James

Everything You Always Wanted to Know About Watergate... But Were Afraid to Ask
with Brian O'Connor

The Insider's Guide to Getting an Agent

Holiday Smut

Superbowl Smut

Happy MILF Day: Stories Celebrating Hot Moms!

Happy DILF Day: Stories Celebrating Hot Dads!

Spanksgiving

Electro Deluxe

Home Alone for Christmas

Women Who Love Monsters

We Love NY: A Romance Anthology

www.ingramcontent.com/pod-product-compliance
Lightning Source LLC
LaVergne TN
LVHW022229200926
848481LV00006B/2181